A Christian Response to Pornography

A Christian Response to Pornography

Shivraj K. Mahendra

2012

A Christian Response to Pornography – Published by the Rev. Dr. Ashish Amos of Indian Society for Promoting Christian Knowledge (ISPCK), Post Box 1585, 1654 Madarsa Road, Kashmere Gate, Delhi-110006.

© Author, 2012
   First Published in 2007
   Second Edition: Revised and Updated, 2012

All rights reserved. No part of this book may be reproduced or transmitted in any form or by any means, electronic, mechanical, photocopying, recording, or by any information storage and retrieval system, without the prior permission in writing from the publisher.

The views expressed in the book are those of the author and the publisher takes no responsibility for any of the statements.

The book in its original form is a thesis submitted to the Senate of Serampore College/University (Union Biblical Seminary, Pune), towards the Bachelor of Divinity degree and is published with written permission (vide PPT/264 29th June 2006; WC/July/06, 11 Sept. 06). The author is responsible for the title, contents and opinions expressed in it.

ISBN: 978-81-8465-247-5

Cover design: Pradeep K.K.

Laser typeset by **ISPCK**, Post Box 1585,
1654 Madarsa Road, Kashmere Gate, Delhi-110006
Tel: 23866322, 23866323
e-mail–ashish@ispck.org.in   • ella@ispck.org.in
website-www.ispck.org.

DEDICATED TO

*All those who are labouring
to liberate the people
struggling with addictions and bondages*

Contents

Dedication	v
Foreword I	ix
Foreword II	xi
Preface to the Second Edition	xiii
Preface to the First Edition	xv
Acknowledgements	xvii
Introduction	**1**
Chapter 1: All About Pornography	**6**
Etymology and Definitions	6
Origin and Developments	9
Appearance and Availability	12
Chapter 2: Global Challenge and Indian Debate	**15**
The Defense of Pornography	16
The Global Phenomena	17
The Indian Scenario	21
The Indian Church on Pornography	29
Chapter 3: Biblical and Theological Response	**32**
The Bible on Pornography	32
A Biblical Theology of Human Sexuality	38
Theology and Pornography	43

Chapter 4:	Ethical Concerns and Reflections	49
	Christian Ethics on Pornography	50
	The Ethics of the Pornographer	59
Chapter 5:	From Bondage to Freedom	60
	The Use of Pornography	60
	Addiction and Effects of Pornography	61
	To those who are in Bondage	68
	To those who are Free	72
	Pastoral Care and Pornography	74
	Towards a Common Response	80

Conclusion	84
Appendices	88
Appendix 1: A Prayer and A Pledge	88
Appendix 2: Check List for Sexual Addiction	90
Appendix 3: Helpful Ministries and Organizations	92
Appendix 4: Suggested Readings	97
Appendix 5: Suggestions for Further Research	98
Bibliography	100

Foreword I

The modern division of theology into separate disciplines of dogmatic, exegetical, historical and systematic theology has sometimes treated areas such as 'ethics' and 'practical theology' as unwanted step-children. However, the early church exemplified a far more healthy and integrative approach to theology. It is, therefore, particularly encouraging to see this important work which demonstrates the necessity of applying theological reflection to the practical issues which we are facing today.

Pornography has become one of the most challenging issues around the world today. In the 16th century the rise of the printing press was accompanied by a dramatic increase in the availability of pornographic materials. Today, with the advent of the internet, the pornographic industry has become a billion dollar enterprise. Tens of thousands of lives and homes are being destroyed through this pernicious evil. This calls for a distinctively Christian response. In this book the author very carefully and systematically sets forth the current state of the problem, along with an excellent biblical and theological response. I commend this book to all. It represents an important application of theological reflection on one of the most important issues facing the church today.

Timothy C. Tennent, Ph.D.
President,
Ausbury Theological Seminary, USA
Former Professor of
World Missions and Indian Studies
Gordon-Conwell Theological Seminary, USA.
Adjunct Professor, New Theological College, Dehra Dun

Foreword II

Mr. Shivraj K. Mahendra deserves appreciation for entering into an area of study and discussion that is apparently forbidden for most Christians both of the pew and the pulpit, let alone the seminarians. I say forbidden because, by definition, pornography means any 'printed or visual material containing the explicit description or display of sexual organs or activity, intended to stimulate erotic rather than aesthetic or emotional feelings.' (*TNOED*). Its origin is from the Greek word '*pornographos*', which means 'writing about prostitutes'. 'What have Christians to do with stuff like these?' one may ask and quite rightly so, if s/he is an innocent church going Christian. But there is a hidden world, both (perhaps) inside and outside the Christian space, in this day and age, that is oblivious to many who do not belong to, or so heavily dependent upon, the current cyber age. It is to this secret world that Mahendra's *A Christian Response to Pornography* attempts to shed some light. He invites us to see this world and challenge it quite seriously. Written originally at the level and scope of a Bachelor of Divinity degree dissertation this book may appear limited in many respects. But surely it is a serious and a bold beginning, a step in the right and perhaps a very needy direction. I along with my colleagues in New Theological College, Dehradun, acclaim Mr. Mahendra for this bold initiative.

Simon Samuel, PhD
Professor of New Testament Studies
Principal, New Theological College, Dehradun

Preface to the Second Edition

It is amazing to see how God uses our small offerings to Him for the greater glory of His Name. I never thought that this little book will call for a second edition! But here it is. Within three years of its publication, all the copies were sold. Since then, a great demand has been coming from all circles – pastors, counselors, theological students, church members, and others.

Meanwhile the book has been awarded the prestigious *ISPCK Author of the Year 2007 Award: The Revd. A. Lobban Award for Christian Indigenous Literature*. It has also, remarkably, secured a place in the *New BD Syllabus (2010) of the Senate of Serampore College (University)*. With such distinctions and pressing demands, I am happily compelled to bring out this revised edition.

Within the limitations of time and resources, I have done as thorough as possible revision of the entire work. Minor corrections and brief additions have been made, apart from updating some information. I am thankful to all who accepted, appreciated and promoted the first edition. Special thanks are due to my dear wife Anita Mahendra, my friend Pastor Ajay Shandilya (Mumbai), and the ISPCK (Delhi) staff for their constant encouragements. It is my prayer that the present edition too will receive a warm acceptance and continue to be a blessing for many.

15 August 2012   Shivraj K. Mahendra
                                         New Theological College,
                                                        Dehradun

Preface to the First Edition

I was challenged to think through the issue of pornography during my recent *theology and ethics* studies. My pursuit began for materials that would help me understand the nature and problem of pornography and provide perspectives and ways to deal with it. I started with Rev. Dr. John Stott's classic *Issues Facing Christians Today*. Having apparently disappointed by it's negligence of the issue and finding no systematic response, particularly from any Indian Christian pen, I was inspired to attempt what you are holding in your precious hands at this moment.

A fruit of more than two years of my research, this book originated actually as a thesis submitted to the Faculty of Union Biblical Seminary, Pune, for the degree of Bachelor of Divinity under the Senate of Serampore College (University). The thesis has been awarded a high first class grade, which, I think, is a due certification to both its quality and relevance.

The original title, *The Issue of Pornography: Theological Response and Ethical Reflections,* has been renamed and some minor changes have been made apart from rewriting select sections. As far as the information on the issue as a whole is concerned, I can hardly claim any originality, and I am greatly indebted to the authors and publishers for their select works and volumes that have helped me construct and reconstruct the contents of this book. Utmost care has been taken to duly acknowledge every citation, quotation or source. However, to err is human!

My commitment to respond to the issue of pornography has taken me through various criticisms, difficulties and discouragements. I have also come across heart-breaking stories of victims as well as inspiring testimonies of those who have won the battle. However, it has not been possible to include everything that was available, keeping the limits of the research and size of the book in mind. Nevertheless, a humble attempt has definitely been made to present the ocean in a drop with a sincere courage to talk about an issue many comfortably shy away from!

I hope and pray that this little book will become a helpful tool in the hands of individuals as well as professionals struggling or dealing with pornography.

For the glory of God,

Shivraj K. Mahendra
NTC, Dehradun
March 6, 2007

Acknowledgements

My prayer and plan to pursue Bachelor of Divinity studies, of which this small book is an outcome, could come true because of the help and support of a number of distinguished individuals whom the Lord brought into my life. In this regard, I am particularly grateful to Dr. Timothy C. Tennent, Rev. George K. Chavanikamannil, Rev. George C. Kuruvilla, and Dr. Simon Samuel and their families.

I am thankful to Anita, my life-partner, for determinedly taking up the double yoke of both our family and her office duty and setting me free from family responsibilities so that I could study. I was able work on this book and complete it successfully because of her constant prayers, support and encouragements.

I would also like to express my thanks to all my teachers and friends at Union Biblical Seminary for their prayers, support and encouragement; especially to Dr. Eliya Mohol and his family, my Care Group and the Hindi Fellowship. Special thanks to Abba Father Prayer Fellowship and friends at New Theological College for their regular prayers during the course of my study. Grateful acknowledgement is also extended to all those who helped in proofreading and editing, especially to Padma and Sharon. The Librarians and staff of The Union Biblical Seminary Library, Pune, The New Theological College Library, Dehradun, and The Jnana Deep Vidya Peeth Library, Pune, deserve special thanks for their help and cooperation.

I would also like to thank Rev. Dr. Ravi Tiwari and other authorities of the Senate of Serampore College for granting me the permission to publish my thesis. I am also grateful to the ISPCK, the publisher of this work, for an excellent job.

Above all, I am grateful to the Lord my God, my Creator and Sustainer, for the gift of life, the privilege of learning, and the opportunity of contributing.

Introduction

Pornography has emerged as a serious threat to the dignity of human sexuality and its divine purpose, challenging the very nature of man and woman and representing the perversion of mind in the contemporary age.

One of the major socio-ethical problems facing the world-society today is pornography. It is widely available and almost everyone has access to it today. Until recently, and to quite a large extent, pornography had been a Western problem! It is with the Internet, VCD/DVD and especially the Mobile revolution that it has become a global phenomenon. We know that the "Internet liberates the word, image and sound from physical constrains and transmits them at a high speed and a low cost."[1] It has helped launch pornography into our everyday life and culture. Tim Berners-Lee, the founder of the Internet, wrote, "The web is more a social creation than a technical one. I designed it for social effect – to help people work together – and not as a technical toy...," and he emphasized that "We have to ensure that the society we build with the web is the sort we intend."[2] Unfortunately, the rampant growth of pornography on the Internet has not helped to create such a society.

---

[1] Rajesh Kochar, "Roving Eye: Coping with Voyeurism in Internet, Digital Technology," *Times of India*, January 22, 2005.

[2] Tim Berners-Lee, *Weaving the Web*, as quoted by Stephen Carrick-Davies "The Whole World in Children's Hands: Pornography, Children and Internet" in Lyndon Bowring, ed., *Searching for Intimacy*, (Bletchley, UK: Authentic Media, 2005), p. 42.

What is pornography? What is it doing to our mind, soul and body? How has it affected our life and behaviour in the society? These are some of the concerns that demand serious reflection. It is to this demand that this book attempts to offer a systematic Christian response.

Human sexuality is a gift of God, created with purpose and dignity. Pornography is a distortion and misrepresentation of sexuality. It has emerged as a serious threat to the dignity of human sexuality and its divine purpose, challenging the very nature of man and woman and representing the perversion of mind in the contemporary age. It has tainted the sanctity and purity of sex, promoted degradation of humanhood and advanced the commercialization of sex, among other things. As a global socio-ethical problem, the issue of pornography needs a systematic analysis and adequate response. In other words, an analysis of the merits, demerits and defenses of pornography is a vital concern of the hour. Is there a framework so as to respond to the issue of pornography theologically? Is it possible to draw some Christian ethical reflections upon this issue in our context? What should our response be to the issue of pornography? The importance of the problem lies in answering these questions. This is high time for us as followers of Christ to respond to the issues challenging the very fabric of our family and society.

There have been ample responses to the issue of pornography from biblical, biological and psychological perspectives in the forms of books, articles in the magazines and awareness programs, in the West.[3]

---

[3] The following works could be mentioned as examples: *Pure Freedom* by Mike Cleveland, *The Silent War* by Henry Rogers, *Pornography: Slaying the Dragon* by David Rowilson, *Think Before You Look* by David Henderson, etc.

Introduction 3

However, the Indian subcontinent has not been able to see any systematic theological and ethical response to the issue. Way back in 1980s India Today[4] made the first attempt (of course, secular) to write about pornography. Now, after several decades, the issue is once again in the air. Since last couple of years secular newspapers as well as news magazines have come up with news, statistics and opinions on the issue of pornography. India Today, The Week, and Outlook are prominent among them.[5] But nothing has come out from the theological and ethical field[6], except for one or two articles in Christian news and family magazines.[7] To be sure, there has been no adequate response to or reflection on the issue in the Indian subcontinent.

---

[4] See, *India Today,* December 15, 1978.

[5] For example, Kanika Gahlaut, "Indian Porn.com" *India Today,* November 8, 2004; Kaveree Bamzai and Sandeep Unnithan, "The Seedy Drive" *India Today,* November 29, 2004; Nikhat Kazmi, "Why Sex Helps Tech Sell..." *Pune Times,* August 2, 2005; Santosh Desai, "The New Pornographies" *The Week,* September 25, 2005. Bollywood producer Mahesh Bhatt's movie, *Kalyug,* is a good attempt toward exposing the dark realities of porn industry. See also, *India Today,* December 5, 2011 (Sex Survey 2011), *Outlook,* December 26, 2011 (Sexual Nirvana) and *India Today,* February 27, 2012 (porn@india).

[6] Much disappointing is John Stott's *Issues Facing Christians Today* which has totally neglected the issue of pornography.

[7] They are, Varun Khare, "Snailed by Pornography" *AIM,* July 2004, pp 16-18; M. Chandrakumar, "How to Overcome Online Temptation" *Light of Life,* August 2004, pp. 45-50; D. James Kennedy and Franklin Graham, "Ten Ways to Break the Stronghold of Pornography" *Forerunner,* June 2005; Duke Jeyaraj, "Hi! I am young and from India: Statistics and Stories that will help one feel the pulse of Indian Youth" *Indian Missions,* Jan-Mar 06, pp.6-14 (Pornography, pp. 11-12), and Dave Breese, " The Downhill Slide" *Confident Living,* March-April 2006.

This book provides a brief introduction to the issue of pornography and then reflecting on the current debates in the world in general and India in particular, it attempts to explore biblical-theological and Christian-ethical responses to it. The book also attempts to provide basic pastoral assistance for rehabilitation of porn victims. In doing all these things, the attempt is to provide perspectives to the seriousness of the problem and conscientize the reader that *prevention is better than cure*. The book does not focus on any case studies or review of the data; rather, it is limited to a general treatment of the issue as a whole from biblical, ethical and pastoral perspectives.

The subject matter of this book is generally organized as per the following descriptions. In the first chapter, we shall see what pornography is all about. Looking at the various definitions of pornography we shall also have a brief note on its origin and development. This chapter will, thus, serve as the stage from where we shall pick up the Indian debate on the issue in the next chapter.

The second chapter, after presenting pornography as a global challenge, will focus on the issue with special reference to India. Inviting select celebrities and their opinions, we shall see if it is okay for India to say "yes" to pornography.

In the third chapter, taking scriptural support from the Bible we shall attempt toward a biblical-theological response to the issue of pornography while reconstructing a Christian theology of human sexuality.

The fourth chapter will concentrate on moral and ethical reflections on the issue of pornography as a whole. Here, select Christian ethical models will be used to critically evaluate the moral and decadent aspects of pornography.

Introduction

Finally, in the fifth and last chapter, having discussed the addiction and effects of pornography, we shall attempt to bring out some rehabilitational concerns providing possible pastoral assistance towards the freedom from addiction to pornography. This chapter will invite persons to give up their willing-slavery to pornography and stand as the victorious children of a Holy and Righteous God.

> *Imagination is a God-given gift; but if it is fed dirt by the eye, it will be dirty. All sin, not least sexual sin, begins with the imagination. Therefore what feeds the imagination is of maximum importance in the pursuit of kingdom righteousness.*
> – D. A. Carson

Chapter 1

All About Pornography

> *To be sure, it is not that the material content of pornography is sexual that is objectionable; rather, it is the manner in which pornography treats sexual matters that makes it unacceptable and discardable.*

Introduction

In this chapter we shall focus on what pornography is all about. Looking at the etymology (word meanings) and select definitions of pornography we shall briefly look into the history of its origin and development. A short discussion on the appearance and availability of pornography is also among the major sections of this chapter. This chapter, thus, serves as the initial platform from where we shall pick up the debate on the issue in the next chapter.

Etymology and Definitions

The word "pornography" (noun) comes from the Greek term *pornographos* (adjective). *Pornographos* is a compound word made of *porni* ("prostitute") and *graphein* ("to write") which means "whore-writing" or "writing about prostitutes." The term is dated around AD 1864.[1] Pornography refers to writings or movies on all kinds of sexual activities outside the bonds of marriage. The term

---

[1] Theodore Pappas, Ed., *Encyclopedia Britannica 2004 Ultimate Reference Suite CD*, Encyclopedia Britannica *Dictionary*, Encyclopedia Britannica, Inc.

"porn" refers to "indecent sexual stuffs" which primarily include "pictures."

The Oxford Advanced Genie defines pornography as books, videos, etc., that describe or show naked people and sexual acts in order to make people feel sexually excited, especially in a way that many other people find offensive.[2] According to Encyclopedia Britannica,

> "... pornography is the representation of erotic behaviour in books, pictures, statues, motion pictures, etc., that is intended to cause sexual excitement. It was originally defined as any work of art or literature depicting the life of prostitutes."[3]

The 1986 Attorney General Commission on Pornography defines pornography as material that is "predominantly sexually explicit and intended primarily for the purpose of sexual arousal."[4]

A detailed definition of pornography will describe it as:

1) a carnal insanity that displays sexual activities predominantly in the form of photographs, motion pictures and writings;
2) a socio-cultural evil that treats human beings as things and women in particular as mere sex objects; and

---

[2] A. S. Hornby, Ed., Oxford Advanced Genie, *Oxford Advanced Learner's Dictionary of Current English*, 6th Edn., (Oxfrod: Oxford University Press, 2000).

[3] Theodore Pappas, Ed., *Encyclopedia Britannica 2004 Ultimate Reference Suite CD*, Encyclopedia Britannica Library, Encyclopedia Britannica, Inc.

[4] Michael McManus, ed., *Final Report of the Attorney General Commission on Pornography*, (Nashville, Tennessee: Rutledge Hill Press, 1986) p. 8 as quoted in J. Kerby Anderson, ed. *Living Ethically in the 90s* (Illinois: Victor Books, 1990) p. 66.

3) the spiritual and ethical blindness which portrays distorted and dehumanized form of sexual activities mostly produced by means of abuse or exploitation.

To speak in one sentence, pornography in essence is a curse to the dignity and sanctity of human sexuality.

Pornography has also been defined as, "the explicit written or visual depiction of living beings, including humans and animals, in sexual acts or fantasies primarily to arouse sexual responses in the reader, viewer or listener."[5]

Another term vital in relation to pornography is obscenity. Obscenity has been legally defined[6] as material which meets following three conditions:

(1) The average person, applying contemporary community standards, would find that the work, taken as a whole, appeals to the prurient interests;

(2) The work depicts or describes, in a patently offensive way, sexual conduct specifically defined by the applicable state (or federal) law, and

(3) The work taken as a whole lacks serious, artistic, political or scientific value.

However, we need to remember that something sexually explicit cannot necessarily be pornographic. Various forms of art and literature would be impoverished by a definition such as this. Also, everything which creates sexual arousal cannot necessarily be pornographic. That would be to include an amazing range of everyday things by which

---

[5] Shiju M. George, "Pornography and Youth," *Revive*, July 2010, p. 8.

[6] Michael McManus, ed., *Final Report of the Attorney General Commission on Pornography*, (Nashville, Tennessee: Rutledge Hill Press, 1986) p. 8.

most persons are not at all aroused, while for some they prove to be very stimulating. To be sure, it is not that the material content of pornography is sexual that is objectionable; rather, it is the manner in which pornography treats sexual matters that makes it unacceptable and discardable. Thus the Lord Longford definition, "Pornography is that which exploits and dehumanizes sex, so that human beings are treated as things and women in particular as sex objects,"[7] more accurately summarizes the challenge of the theme we are attempting to dealing here with.

Origin and Developments

Not much is known about the origins[8] and earliest forms of pornography. One assumed reason for this is that it was customarily not considered worthy of transmission or preservation. First documented pornographic pictures were printed in oriental manuals of sex, Kama Sutra was the most popular one among them. The Hindus feared that the paper works would not survive and decorated the temples of Khajuraho (India) with numerous figurines of people having sex.[9] The first clear historical evidences of pornography in Western culture has been found in the sensational songs performed in ancient Greece at festivals

---

[7] Lord Longford, *Pornography: The Longford Report*, (London: Coronet Books, 1972) p. 412 as quoted in John H. Court, *Pornography: A Christian Critique* (Illinois: InterVarsity Press, 1980), p. 10.

[8] For the information on this section I have largely depended on the *Encyclopedia Britannica 2004 Ultimate Reference Suite CD*, Encyclopedia Britannica, Inc., to which I duly acknowledge my indebtedness. I shall attempt to explore the origin and development of pornography in India in Chapter #2.

[9] "History of pornography: scandalous beginning and habitual reality" Available at http://english.pravda.ru/society/sex/11-07-2007/94805-pornography-0/ (Accessed on 1 June 2012).

honouring the god Dionysius. Indisputable evidence of graphic pornography in Roman culture is found at Pompeii, where erotic paintings dating from the 1st century AD cover walls sacred to bacchanalian orgies.[10] A classic of written pornography is said to be the Roman poet Ovid's *Arsamatoria* (Art of Love). This is a treatise on the art of seduction, intrigue, and sensual arousal.

During the Middle Ages[11] pornography was widespread in Europe. But it was held in low repute, expressed mostly in riddles, common jokes, doggerel, and satirical verses. A notable exception is the Decameron of Giovanni Boccaccio,[12] some of whose 100 stories are licentious in nature. A principal theme of medieval pornography was the sexual license of monks and other clerics, along with their attendant displays of hypocrisy.

With the invention of printing press took place the rebirth of ambitious pornographic written works. These writings frequently contained elements of humour and romance. They were written to entertain as well as to arouse. Many of these works reminded back to classical writings in their treatment of the joys and sorrows of marital deception and infidelity.

The first modern pornographic works that were both devoid of literary value and designed solely to arouse sexual excitement appeared in Europe in the 18th century. A small underground traffic in such works became the

---

[10] Festivals of god Dionysius.

[11] The period in European history from the collapse of Roman civilization in the 5th century C.E. to the period of the Renaissance.

[12] Giovanni Boccaccio (A.D. 1313-1375), an Italian poet and scholar, is best remembered as the author of the earthy tales in the Decameron. With Petrarch he laid the foundations for the humanism of the Renaissance and raised vernacular literature to the level and status of the classics of antiquity.

basis of a separate publishing and bookselling business in England. A classic of this period was the widely read *Fanny Hill*; or, *Memoirs of a Woman of Pleasure* (1749) by John Cleland. At about this time erotic graphic art began to be widely produced in Paris, eventually coming to be known as French postcards.

Pornography, both in books and pictures, flourished in the Victorian era despite, or perhaps because of the prevailing taboos on sexual topics. In 1834 an investigation in London established the presence of 57 pornographic shops on Holywell Street (Oxford) alone. A notable work of Victorian pornography is the massive and anonymous autobiography *My Secret Life* (1890), which is both a social chronicle of the underside of a Puritanical society and a minutely detailed recounting of one English gentleman's lifelong pursuit of sexual gratification. According to Graham-Murray never before or since has there existed such a large number of prostitutes (in proportion to the population size) as during the Victorian age.[13]

The development of photography and later on motion pictures contributed greatly to the proliferation of pornographic materials. Throughout the ages pornography has evolved and developed, but it was not until the technological and ideological progress of the 20th century that pornography was able to find its way in literally every aspect of modern society.[14] Pornography in the 20th century was unprecedented in the variety of media used and the enormous volume of works produced. Since World War II, written pornography has been largely superseded by explicit visual representations of erotic behaviour that

---

[13] James Graham-Murray, *A History of Morals* (London: Library 33 Limited, 1966), p. 149.

[14] Alex, "History of Pornography, and How it Became a Problem," Available at http://www.feedtherightwolf.org/2011/07/history-of-pornagraphy-and-how-it/ (Accessed on 1 June 2012).

are considered lacking in redeeming artistic or social values. And today at the dawn of the 21st century one can see with the breakthrough of Internet how the delivery of pornography has become revolutionized.

Appearance and Availability

The two common forms of pornography are soft core and hard core. Soft core pornography features naked or scantily clothed men and women. It highlights breasts and genitalia but shows no sexual intercourse. It does not emphasize violence or sexual perversion.[15] It is said that soft core pornography is not illegal.[16] Much of the advertisements today could easily be kept in this category.

On the other hand, hard core pornography includes various forms of sexual penetration, forced or unforced, between two or more people.[17] It has no restriction or limitation. Human depravity can be portrayed in any setting. Torture, horrifying killings, and all kinds of perverted sexual activities are promoted in the world of "hard core".[18]

For many years, both soft-core as well as hard-core pornography have been made widely available in adult magazines (photographs), videocassettes (now VCDs and

---

[15] Alice Swann, "The Role of Pornographic Industry in the Destruction of Intimacy" in Lyndon Bowring, ed., *Searching for Intimacy*, (Bletchley, UK: Authentic Media, 2005), p. 5.

[16] David Hocking, *The Moral Catastrophe*, (Oregon: Harvest House Publishers, 1990), p. 101.

[17] Jeff Olson, *When A Man's Eye Wanders*, (Grand Rapids: RBC Ministries, 1999), p. 4.

[18] David Hocking, *The Moral Catastrophe*, (Oregon: Harvest House Publishers, 1990), p. 101. See also, Alice Swann, "The Role of Pornographic Industry in the Destruction of Intimacy" in Lyndon Bowring, ed., *Searching for Intimacy*, (Bletchle, UK: Authentic Media, 2005), p. 5.

DVDs), motion pictures, and television. Today there are also audio porn ("Dial-a-Porn," Hot Talks, etc.) and porn on mobile phones (via MMS etc). But with the enhancement of Internet a revolution in the delivery of pornography has come about and the Internet has become the most commonly accessible means to pornographic gratification. It has got photographs, videos, voice-porn, live-porn, etc., in all categories and great varieties. Everything you imagine, its there!

Playboy, *Penthouse* and *Hustler* have been the most popular magazines in the history of pornography. Traditionally each brand has dominated a specific niche within the men's magazine market; *Playboy* is known for its softcore content, *Hustler* is known for its hardcore material, and *Penthouse* occupies the space in-between. Men's magazines were the primary vehicle for pornographic distribution from the early twentieth century to the 1970s. Their popularity declined alongside the advent of new technologies.[19]

While the appearance and availability of pornography may suggest it to be purely an adult phenomenon, it is not so. Child pornography, as a serious form of child abuse, pictures children being sexually exploited and tortured by adults. The abuse can include exhibitionism, obscene talking in addition to fondling, vaginal, oral or anal sex. Though girl children are noted to be the main victims, boy children too are abused. Child pornography shows various sexual activities including penetrative sex between a child and an adult. Child pornography had become a multimillion-dollar international industry by the mid-1970s. To deal with it, governments have passed laws

---

[19] "The History of Modern Pornography" Available at http://www.pornographyhistory.com/(Accessed on 1 June 2012).

making it a felony punishable by heavy fines and jail sentences.[20] Yet there are more than 116,000 Daily "child pornography" requests on the Internet and more than 100,000 websites that offer illegal child pornography.[21]

Summary

In this chapter we have seen in general, the information on what pornography is all about. We are now familiar with the terminology, origin and historic development of pornography through the centuries. Having acquainted ourselves with the basics in the issue of pornography we shall now engage ourselves with the contemporary debate in the next chapter.

> *Pornography is that which exploits and dehumanizes sex, so that human beings are treated as things and women in particular as sex objects.*

---

[20] *Compton's Interactive Encyclopedia Deluxe* © 1998 The Learning Company, Inc.

[21] For current statistics, log on to, *http://internet-filter-review.toptenreviews.com/internet-pornography-statistics.html/* (Accessed on 28 May 2012).

Chapter 2

Global Challenge and Indian Debate

> *Pornography is a market-driven industry. Laws remain insufficient and churches have much to do to fight against the rampant growth of this global social evil.*

Introduction

As stated previously, pornography has been, until recently, more of a western phenomenon.[1] The Indian subcontinent is now facing this problem like never before. It is not that India has been unaware or innocent of pornography,[2] but with the growth of Internet, CDs and Mobiles, a revolution has taken place in the delivery and consumption of pornography. And the task of this chapter is to focus on the issue of pornography with special reference to India. Also, a general survey of the global phenomena and legal matters related to pornography shall add to the contents of this chapter. Inviting various celebrities we shall see if it is okay for India to say "yes" to pornography. Finally, the chapter will highlight the response of the Church to the issue in focus. We shall begin with a note on the defense of pornography.

---

[1] "Western" in terms of greater production, proliferation, consumption and sponsorship; referring mainly to the USA and the European contexts.

[2] To be sure, the history of the Indian culture and literature has much to tell us about pornography in India as we shall see under section titled, The Indian Scenario.

The Defense of Pornography

In spite of its explicit harmful effects, which we shall see ahead, pornography has been defended from various points of view. Following is a summarized list of the major defenses of pornography.

According to the so called Evidence Argument[3], pornography has no effect upon a person's character and that it is not harmful. The Therapeutic Argument believes that pornography can help overcome various sexual problems including frigidity and impotence.[4] The Social Benefit Argument holds that legalizing pornography can reduce sex crimes and porn market.[5] The Moral-inversion Argument attempts to present alternative to traditional morality by replacing love with hatred, by deforming what is beautiful and praising ugliness.[6] Similarly, the Ideological and Liberation arguments believe that pornography can serve as a vehicle to overthrow the old repressive culture, the coldness of the anti-sexual philosophy of traditional morality.[7] Finally, the Civil Liberties Argument defends pornography as part of the issue of the freedom of speech.[8]

These defenses add to the challenges of pornography demanding serious response. We will be responding to these challenges in the subsequent topics and chapters. Meanwhile, look at this self contradicting defense of pornography.

---

[3] The American *Presidential Commission Report on Obscenity and Pornography, 1970.* See, John H. Court, *Pornography: A Christian Critique,* (Illinois: InterVarsity Press, 1980), pp. 13-16.

[4] John H. Court, *Pornography: A Christian Critique,* pp. 16-17.

[5] John H. Court, *Pornography: A Christian Critique,* pp. 17-18.

[6] John H. Court, *Pornography: A Christian Critique,* pp. 20-23.

[7] John H. Court, *Pornography: A Christian Critique,* pp. 23-28.

[8] John H. Court, *Pornography: A Christian Critique,* pp. 28-29.

"The Good of Porn"

In the article "The Naked Truth", Nona Walia almost defends pornography by highlighting *the good of porn* in following terms:

> "If you are watching porn for fun, it can excite and energise your sex life; Porn can help you understand your sexual desires and help communicate your physical needs better; and, Its visual imagery can give an intellectual spark to fashion designers, writers, filmmakers and creative people."[9]

Interestingly, author's own remark in the same article, contradicts this view, when Walia rightly affirms, "You can't learn the truth about sex from pornography. It doesn't deal in truth. Pornography is not meant to educate, but to sell."

The Global Phenomena

This section provides us with world pornography statistics. The attempt here is to present in brief the gigantic structure of porn industry, its massive production, huge revenue and groups of consumer-victims. Thus, the section gives us a glance of pornography as a global challenge today.

Production and Consumption[10]

Revenue. The size of the pornography industry worldwide is reported to be of more than 60 billion US dollars.[11] Out

---

[9] Nona Walia, "The Naked Truth," *Times Life: A Supplement to Sunday Times of India,* Pune, August 29, 2004.

[10] The details of this section are largely based on the information available at, http://www.internet-filter-review toptenreviews.com/ internet-pornography-statistics.html/ (Accessed: November 6, 2005, revisited on 28 May 2012). Kindly log on to this site for current updates and latest figures.

[11] For latest figures, kindly visit http://www.internet-filter-review.toptenreviews.com/ internet-pornography-statistics.html/ (Thank You).

of this, $20 billion comes from Adult Videos, $11 billion from Escort services, $7.5 billion from Magazines, $5 billion from Sex Clubs, $2.5 billion from Internet and $1.5 billion from CD-ROM. Notably, porn revenue is larger than all combined revenues of all professional football, baseball and basketball franchises. Pornography also turns a larger profit than the conventional film and music industries combined.

Internet. There are more than 4.2 million pornographic websites, which is 12% of the total websites. The worldwide visitors to pornographic websites number 72 million annually. Daily pornographic search engine requests are 68 million, which is 25% of total search engine requests. Monthly pornographic downloads number 1.5 billion, this is 35% of all the downloads.

Children and Teenagers. The average age of first Internet exposure to pornography is reported to be 11 years old. Largest consumer of Internet pornography belongs to the 12-17 age groups. Also, 80% of 15-17 year olds are reported to have multiple hard-core exposures. Almost 90% of 8-16 year olds have viewed porn online, most while doing their homework.

Men. The total number of men admitting to accessing pornography at work is 20%. It is reported that 40 million US adults regularly visit Internet pornography websites. There are 47% Christians who said pornography is a major problem in the home. Adults admitting to Internet sexual addiction number 10%. The breakdown of male/female visitors to pornography sites is: 72% male - 28% female.

Women. It is reported that 70% of women keep their cyber activities secret. 17% of all women struggle with pornography addiction. Women favor chat rooms twice more than men. Every 1 out of 3 visitors to all adult websites is woman. Each month 9.4 million women are said to access adult websites. Women admitting to accessing pornography at work number 13% of all working women.

The Response of the Nation States

Several nation states have responded to the issue of pornography with notably different approaches, although basically on legal grounds. Denmark has legalized porn way back in 1960s. For producers of sex films, everything is legal in this nation. Glowing computer screens and super-fast broadband connections create a lot of money for adult webmasters in Sweden. Norway is a gold mine for live-shows and pay-sites. Special shipping rules are in place in the country. New Zealand has a well-built, vigorous and vivacious sex industry. It is constantly changing to keep up with the times. In the United States of America the only explicit, hard-core sexual material that is absolutely illegal by law today is child pornography. Pornography as such is not illegal in the United Kingdom. It becomes unlawful if and when it qualifies as being obscene according to the Obscene Publications Act of 1959. The legal test of obscenity is the 'depravity and corruption' measure.[12] Pornography is declared a human right for British prisoners.[13]

The Response of the Churches and Organizations

The Catholic Church, drawing on natural law theology, has condemned pornography as undermining human dignity and subverting the common social good. According to the Pontifical Council for Social Communications,

---

[12] Nikhat Kazmi & Allen O'brien, "Legalise Porn?" *Times News Network*, Tuesday, July 12, 2005.

[13] Complete news can be found at http://www.telegraph.co.uk/news/uknews/1412742/Prisoners-win-their-claim-that-hardcore-porn-is-a-human-right.html (Reaccessed on 28 May 2012).

> "Pornography and sadistic violence debase sexuality, corrode human relationships, exploit individuals – especially women and young people, undermine marriage and family life, foster anti-social behaviour and weaken the moral fibre of society itself."[14]

The Pope has called for effective laws preventing broadcasters and publishers from exploiting sex and the repetition of evil."[15] The Catholic Church as a whole feels the need of a strong, clear call to battle in defense of chastity and raising up of moral leadership in every diocese.

In one of its resolutions on the issue, the Episcopal Church has called for stricter and tougher enforcement of already existing laws against pornography. The Presbyterian Church and the American Lutheran Church have condemned the proliferation of sexually explicit materials that demean men and women. We see that both mainline Protestant and Catholic churches have been addressing the issue.[16] Some denominations, such as the Southern Baptist Convention, the Evangelical Lutheran Church in America and the United Methodist Church, have expressed special outrage particularly over child pornography. Also, the United Church of Canada has created a new statement, responding largely to issues in relation to sexual violence.

---

[14] Pontifical Council for Social Communications, *Pornography and Violence in the Communication Media: a Pastoral Response*, 7 May 1989 (Vatican Polyglot Press, 1989), nr. 10 as quoted in Karl H. Peschke, *Christian Ethics: Moral Theologies in the Light of Vatican II, Vol. 2* (Bangalore: Theological Publication in India, 2004), p. 441.

[15] Paul J. Murphy, "Pornography and the Church," *Homiletic and Pastoral Review*, November 1990, pp. 60-62.

[16] See the article, "Censorship or Education? Feminist Views on Pornography" by Mary Ellen Ross at http://www.religion-online.org/

The Lambeth Conference of 1988 viewed promiscuity, adultery, prostitution, and pornography, etc. as sinful and opposed to the Christian way of life. The Statement of the Conference reads, "From a Christian perspective, these forms of sexual expression remain sinful, how much some elements of secular societies seek to justify them."[17]

Ecumenical leaders in states such as Pennsylvania have joined to oppose pornography. Evangelical groups, for instance, the National Coalition Against Pornography (NCAP), are claiming a growing membership and using activist strategies. The Religious Alliance Against Pornography (RAAP) is composed of both liberals and conservatives. It has sponsored a White House Conference and has begun organizing local groups around the country. The National Council of Churches of Christ (NCCC) has suggested that the churches give "priority attention" to the "glut of violence and sexual violence" in the media.[18]

The Indian Scenario

According to short a survey personally conducted by the author, most rural folks in India enjoy access to pornography through VCD/DVD, Magazines, occasionally the Internet, and of course Mobiles. Thus, surprisingly, the porn fever is not limited only to urban contexts, as might be considered. Though much material has reportedly been *videshi*, Bollywood[19] has not contributed less to the proliferation of pornography in

---

[17] Lambeth Document on Human Sexuality (p. 20), as quoted in George Mathew Nalunnakkal, "The Indian Church and the Sacred Cow of Human Sexuality" *National Council of Churches Review*, May 2001, p. 327.

[18] Mary Pellauer, "Pornography: An Agenda for the Churches", at http://www.religion-online.org/ (Accessed: November 6, 2005).

[19] Videshi = foreign, Bollywood = The Mumbai Film Industry.

India. Also, there is said to be both independent as well as sponsored production of pornographic stuff in recent years. The metropolis of Chennai, along with Delhi and Mumbai, has been noticed as one of the key porn industries in the nation.[20] But looking at the past, none of these should surprise us.

The Past and the Present

Ancient India was surprisingly open on issues related to sex and sexuality. We have innumerable temples depicting erotic as well as pornographic images of all kinds of sexuality practiced by humans, gods and goddesses.[21] Distinguished literatures and religious volumes such as *Kama Sutra, Ramayana, Upanishadas* and *Puranas* are worth mentioning at this point.

The *Kama Sutra* (Aphorisms on Sexual Love) of Vatsyaayana is a book containing detailed instructions on sexual activities and methods. It is the first literary classic in the world on the matters of sex. It was written in the early part of the Christian era (c. AD 4th Century) and is still looked at with admiration by the West. The *Kama Sutra* teaches that the final aim of sexual pleasure is spiritual, and that like ethics and prosperity, sexuality is one of the bases of civilization. It also delinks sexual pleasure from procreation, emphasizing that procreation is not the aim of sexual love. According to D. Alain,

---

[20] The City of Pune is said to rank third in terms of cyber crimes in India. Adult porn is the biggest component of cyber crime. See, Nikhat Kazmi, "Why Sex Helps Tech Sell..." *Pune Times, The Times of India,* Tuesday, August 2, 2005, p.1. For Sexual Revotution in Asia, see, Pater Lane, *Setting the Captives Free* (Milton, Australia: Exodus Asia Pacific, 2005), pp. 9-17.

[21] For example, the Chandela temples of Khajuraho in central India built in the tenth century C.E. Contain stunningly sexually explicit sculptures.

"amorous ecstasy is assimilated to mystic experience, to the perception of the divine that is supreme enjoyment."[22] Generally considered to be a great work of erotica, *Kama Sutra* also appears to be a striking literature of pornography.

It will be shocking for many to know that, according to Dr. Chatterjee, pornography is replete in the *Ramayana*, especially in the older unedited versions.[23] The descriptions of sexual activities of the *Ramayana*-society, it is said, are so explicit that they cross the boundary of erotica.[24] *Upanishadas* and *Puranas* too provide details on sexuality and sexual activities. There are a lot of stories of sexual activities of gods and goddesses in these literatures.[25] Thus one can find a great history of erotica and pornography in India where both temple arts and religious literatures are characterized, to a great extent, with pornographic elements in their contents, nature of appearance and descriptions.[26]

---

[22] Danielou Alain, translator, *The complete Kama Sutra, the first Modern Translation of the Classic Indian Text* (Vermont: Park Street Press, 1994), pp. 10-34.

[23] Chatterjee, "Pornography in Ramayana", http://www.dalitstan.org/books/awake/awake4.html/ (Accessed: October 29, 2005). Also available at, http://www.angelfire.com/journal/wrote/Awake3.html (Accessed on 28 May 2012). Scholars say that the popular versions of Ramayan are carefully edited and do not contain obscene details.

[24] For a detailed discussion on this issue, see, Ananda Guruge, *The Society of the Ramayana*, (New Delhi: Abhinav Publications, 1991), pp. 184-216.

[25] A major part of the *Brahmavaivart Purana* and select portions of the *Rigveda* contain great descriptions of sexual acts which appear to be explicitly pornographic (e.g., Rigveda 1.28.2; and 10.85.37 etc.). Detailed illustrations can be found in, Harimohan Jha, *Khattar Kaka*, (New Delhi: Rajkamal Prakashan, 2001), pp. 216-236.

[26] See also, George Mathew Nalunnakkal, "The Indian Church and the Sacred Cow of Human Sexuality" *National Council of Churches Review*, May 2001, pp. 323-325.

However, the Indian society in general has also honoured sex as something sacred and divine. Sex has been treated as something really private or as, *parde ki cheej*, a thing of curtain. There was a time when women were respected as *Devis* and *Lakshmis*. Today their identity seems to be limited (or being limited) to that of mere sex symbols, unfortunately! The time has changed significantly! Or perhaps a reverse of time is at hand!

Reflecting on the present scenario, we find Indian movie makers have been increasingly looking for ways to bring more nudity and more sexual shock-values into their films, even taking time to recruit actors and actresses with these particular skills.[27] They are researching American adult movie methods and techniques to assist in the production of Bollywood's own versions. This though raises the question of when does a film become pornographic or when is it erotic. To be sure, while erotica encapsules the embodiment of wanting of desire, an invitation to go on a journey of exploration, pornography is nothing more than a stripped down version which will take persons into a void and it removes any pleasure and eventually suffocates love. Erotica or the Erotic is a positive element in life experience; it is not as pornography, a negative and destructive one![28]

The Law and the Punishment

Under Section 292 of the Indian Penal Code (IPC), "any material which is lascivious or appeals to the prurient interest or if its effect is such as to tend to deprave and corrupt persons who view it," is pornography. And if

---

[27] See, Bharati K. Dubey, "Indian Society Comes To Terms With Sex Sleaze," *The Movie Age*, August 6, 2004, p.1.

[28] Further discussion related to this section continue in the section on celebrity opinions below.

caught purchasing, sending, publishing or creating pornography, you are in for at least a two-year jail sentence and or a minimum Rs. 2,000.00 fine.

According to Section 67 of the Information Technology (IT) Act 2000,

> "Whoever publishes or transmits or causes to be published in the electronic form any material which is lascivious or appeals to the prurient interest or if its effect is such as to tend of deprave or corrupt persons who are likely, having regard to all relevant circumstances, to read, see or hear the matter contained or embodied in it, shall be punished on first conviction with imprisonment of either description or a term which may extend to Five Years and with fine which may extend to One Lakh rupees and in the event of a second or a subsequent conviction with imprisonment of either description of a term which may extent to Ten Years and also with fine which may extend to Two Lakh rupees."[29]

It may be noticed that watching or consuming pornography is not an offence as per the above law. All that the law forbids is the publication or transmission of pornographic material. "Consumption of pornography on a personal device is frowned upon by neither the Victorian-vintage Indian Penal Code (IPC) nor the 21st Century Legislation on Information Technology", says journalist Manoj Mitta.[30] Both laws, separated by over 130 years, are unsparing towards the producer or supplier of obscene

---

[29] Quoted from Sahayog India: http://www.sahayogindia.org/ (Accessed on 15 January 2006).

[30] Manoj Mitta, "Watching Pornography No Offence: IPC and IT Act" *Times of India,* May 28, 2011, online version, http://articles.timesofindia.indiatimes.com/2011-05-28/india/29594374_1_pornography-obscene-material-section-67b (Accessed on 28 May 2012).

material. But when it comes to the consumer, neither law offers any scope to the police to make out even the lesser charge of abetting the alleged crime of obscenity. It is just as well that the laws are not prudish about consumption per se because mobiles have of late emerged as a major medium for pornography around the world.[31] Mobiles can now match the capability of laptops in showing long videos of pornography, with the added advantage of offering greater privacy.

Unfortunately the government or the law can do nothing about this. In a recent amendment to the Information Technology (IT) Act 2000, the government has given up the power to block pornographic websites purely on the ground of obscenity. Now, the courts alone can block such sites. This is because Section 69A, which came into effect on October 27, 2009 has raised the bar for the executive power to block porn websites. The government can still block such websites, but only if they create a "public order" problem, which is an unlikely probability.

Is It Okay If India Says Yes?

With the above brief survey of the past, a note on the law and contemporary question on the issue, we now turn to various opinions on pornography in India.

Celebrity and Media Opinions. Salman Rushdie,[32] in a recent pornography book, *XXX: 30 Porn Star,* has argued that porn is vital to freedom and that free and civilized

---

[31] Manoj Mitta, "Watching Pornography No Offence: IPC and IT Act."

[32] Born in India, Rushdie lived in England for many years and the British spent more than 10 million pounds to protect him from the Ayatollah Khomeini's fatwa condemning him to death for authoring *The Satanic Verses.* He currently lives in New York.

societies should be judged by their willingness to accept such materials.[33] He says pornography exists everywhere, but when it comes into societies in which it is difficult for young men and women to get together and do what young men and women often like doing, it satisfies a more general need.[34]

On the one hand a host of celebrities have enthusiastically endorsed Rushdie's view. For example, to theatre personality, Alyque Padamsee, porn is okay because India is the land of the erotic. According to him celeb porn is eroticized male and female fantasy and there is nothing wrong with that. However, he is against all forms of child pornography.

Actor Aly Khan thinks that pornography is literature and it should be available to people in a free society, although it should be censored so that children don't have access to it. To him, banning it will be like banning literature. To socialite Pooja Bedi, it is healthy to be exposed to sex and pornography and to the sexual process at the right age and you have to be mentally ready for it. She agrees that we must be open about sexuality and be able to see porn if we want.

On the other hand some celebrities do have anti-porn opinions. According to author Shobha De, Salman Rushdie has made a living out of being controversial and she isn't surprised by his statement. She finds porn very disgusting and thinks that it propagates an abnormal idea of sex. There are several others who find pornography as problematic and abhorrent because it portrays violence and domination in a sexual context.

---

[33] *The Daily Mail*, London, August 14, 2004; Visit also, http://www.traditionalvalues.org/ (Accessed on 15 January 2006).

[34] For additional and latest details you may log on to, http://www.*AsianSexGazette.com/ (Accessed on 15 January 2006).*

Sunday Debate of the *Times of India* brings face to face its Associate Editor Jug Suraiya and Senior Assistant Editor Vikas Singh on "Is Pornography a touchstone of a free society?" To Suraiya the answer is "No." According to him,

> "The bare truth about pornography is that far from being a liberating influence – as Rushdie and others claim – it is an instrument of exploitation and imprisionment. It represents an impoverishment of our sexual imagination. Let's not confuse... pornography with erotica."[35]

In contrast, Vikas Singh opines,

> "We may find pornography vile and repulsive, in which case we are free to shun it. But does that give us the right to dictate to others what they should do and how they should think? ... One person's art is another's pornography."[36]

Singh is apparently unaware of the dark side of pornography and falsely sees it as an empowering choice and a price of freedom!

Is It Time To Legalize Porn In India? Cyber law expert Pavan Duggal's answer is "Yes!"[37] According to model Upen Patel, as long as we do not intrude on anyone's privacy, watching porn should have nothing to do with the law. Theatre personality Rahul DaCunha thinks that legalizing porn will make society much cleaner and much more normal. He says "It's available anyway, so legalize it."[38]

---

[35] See, *Sunday Times of India*, Pune, August 15, 2004, p.8.

[36] See, *Sunday Times of India*, Pune, August 15, 2004, p.8.

[37] Nikhat K azmi & Allen O'brien, "Legalise Porn?" *Times News Network*, Tuesday, July 12, 2005.

[38] Nikhat K azmi & Allen O'brien, "Legalise Porn?" *Times News Network*, Tuesday, July 12, 2005.

Photographer Atul Kasbekar says that we can't pretend we are living in a safer society if we make porn legal. Shobha De is against institutionalizing porn. She asserts, "We have seen repercussions in so-called developed countries like Sweden or Norway and I don't think legalizing porn solves the problem."[39] To be sure, legalizing porn in several countries has only resulted in greater proliferation of the porn market and pornography has been the key in almost every sex crime.[40] This is a clear refutation of the Social Benefit Argument, which holds that legalizing pornography can reduce sex crimes and porn market.[41]

The Indian Church on Pornography

Sexuality is one of the most sensitive and difficult issues that confronts the Church in India today. For most, or almost all, the churches in our country it is still a taboo to talk about sex and sexual issues.[42] The churches in India have not yet come up with any official statements related to the issues of human sexuality, particularly that of pornography. Whatever is available are some casual announcements on behalf of some churches or some ecumenical forums that also on certain issues like marriage bills and divorce laws. For example, the National Council of Churches in India has dedicated the May 2001 issue of its monthly magazine, *National Council of Churches Review*,

---

[39] Nikhat Kazmi & Allen O'brien, "Legalise Porn?" *Times News Network*, Tuesday, July 12, 2005.

[40] For details and latest examples, log on to, http://www.obscenitycrimes.org/ or related links.

[41] John H. Court, *Pornography: A Christian Critique*, (Illinois: InterVarsity Press, 1980), pp. 17-18, 48-53.

[42] For an underlining of the opinion, see, George Mathew Nalunnakkal, "The Indian Church and the Sacred Cow of Human Sexuality" *National Council of Churches Review*, May 2001, p. 321.

to the issue of human sexuality particularly dealing with the issue of homosexuality. Sadly, the issue of pornography is untouched.

Some individuals, however, have definitely tried to reflect on the issue.[43] Yet nothing has come out from the theological-ethical circle. Thus, there is no official and or systematic response to the issue of pornography from the Indian Church. One of the chief reasons why the Indian Church is still hesitant to talk about sexuality and issues related to it, is because it still considers sex as a sensitive concern. In order for the church to address human sexuality seriously, it has to understand sexuality as a divinely ordained nature. It needs to treat sexual issues as religio-theological issues. Therefore, the challenge and focus of this study is to respond to the issue of pornography from an Indian Christian perspective.

Summary

In this chapter we have seen the world pornography statistics. We have seen pornography as a global challenge and the responses of different nations, churches and organizations to it. In addition, we have seen some of the defenses of pornography and legal matters relating to the issue, in this chapter. Having visited the Indian history on sexuality in brief, we have also noticed what various celebrities in our own country have to say about the issue. Pornography is a market-driven industry. Laws remain insufficient and churches have much to do to fight against the rampant growth of this global social evil. The Indian debate of whether pornography is alright remains without conclusion and a Christian response is a challenge and

---

[43] For example, Varun Khare, "Snailed by Pornography" *AIM*, July 2004, pp 16-18; and M. Chandrakumar, "How to Overcome Online Temptation" *Light of Life*, August 2004, pp. 45-50.

an imperative of the hour. The book, therefore, engages towards a candid biblical and theological response to the issue of pornography in the following chapter.

> *Pornography and sadistic violence debase sexuality, corrode human relationships, exploit individuals – especially women and young people, undermine marriage and family life, foster anti-social behaviour and weaken the moral fibre of society itself.*

Chapter 3

Biblical and Theological Response

> *Human sexuality is a gift of God but pornography distorts and misrepresents this gift. It is against the Biblical purposes of sexuality, and thus it is anti-life and anti-God.*

Introduction

A Christian response to any issue facing the Church today has to be, unquestionably, a biblical-theological one. The Bible is the basis on which every Christian opinion is to be based. It is God's Word to humanity providing instructions for godly living. Thus an Indian Christian response to the issue we are dealing here with has to be derived from the Word of God. The task of this chapter, therefore, is to explore a biblical and theological response to the issue of pornography.

The Bible on Pornography

It is not impossible that at the time when the Bible was written there were various art forms that depicted sexually explicit things. But apparently this phenomenon of pornography was not sufficiently prevalent enough to be addressed in the Bible. However, we can surely underscore a wide range of biblical passages that establish the limits of appropriate sexual conduct and are significantly relevant to the issue of pornography.

"Pornography" in the Bible

While the English word "pornography" is not found in the Bible, it is included in such words as lasciviousness, wantonness and licentiousness. In fact, the word "fornication" comes from the Greek word *porneia* from which we get the English word "pornography." *Porneia* includes sexual immorality of all kinds. The Bible translates this word as "sexual immorality." *Porneuo* is the verb meaning "to commit fornication (adultery)." We read in the Bible, the Lord Jesus said,

> "But I say to you that whoever divorces his wife for any reason except sexual immorality causes her to commit adultery; and whoever marries a woman who is divorced commits adultery." (Matthew 5:32 NKJV).[1]

We also read Apostle Paul, saying, "Foods for the stomach and the stomach for foods, but God will destroy both it and them. Now the body is not for sexual immorality but for the Lord, and the Lord for the body... Flee sexual immorality. Every sin that a man does is outside the body, but he who commits sexual immorality sins against his own body." (1 Corinthians 6:13 and 18 NKJV).

Fornication or adultery is generally described as 'sexual intercourse outside of marriage', but the biblical meaning is significantly wider. Apostle Paul could have meant one of the three things when he used the term *porneuo*:[2]

(1) *to prostitute one's body to satisfy the lust of another;*

(2) *to have 'illicit' or 'unlawful' sexual intercourse.* E.g., as adultery, premarital sex, homosexuality and lesbianism, as bestiality, or as incest, etc.; and

---

[1] See also, Romans 1: 28-30.
[2] See, 1 Corinthians 10:8.

(3) *idolatry* - not just worship of images, but allowing one's self to be drawn to anything.

Men do not escape this condemnation, as may be thought, for the masculine form, on which *porne* is rooted, is *pornos*. It means fornicator or whoremonger: a male prostitute or a man who indulges in illicit and immoral sexual behaviour.

A Biblical Response to Pornography

Pornography or sexual immorality is considered to be more disgusting than any other sexual evil in the Bible. Both the Old Testament and the New Testament have strong resentments towards the issue of sexual immorality and they condemn every form of pornographic perversion in relation to sexual behavior.

The Old Testament. In the Old Testament Yahweh (God) prescribed Israel's worship, which was clearly not to be associated with temple prostitution.[3] In Deuteronomy 23:17 sacred prostitution is unequivocally denied a place in Israel's worship. In the worship of Israel, cultic prostitution was regarded in the same way as sexual promiscuity with prostitutes (Hebrew *zunot*). Not only was that wrong in itself, but even the money earned through acts of prostitution would not be acceptable as payment for a vow to the Lord (Deuteronomy 23:18).

Prostitution, in general, was punishable by death. So also were a series of other types of promiscuous and incestuous sexual acts (pornographic practices!). While the women were severely punished for promiscuity, it

---

[3] Semitic religious practices regarded the divine love-making as a solemn act. It therefore behooved the Canaanites to imitate the gods Baal and Asherah by practicing temple prostitution in order to maintain the seasonal cycle.

seems as though men were condoned for being lured by lewd women (Genesis 38:12-26; Joshua 2). However, prostitution was shunned and this is why the classical prophets referred to Israel's apostasy as harlotry or prostitution (Hosea 1-3; Ezekiel 16; 23).[4] Hosea paints a negative or pornographic picture of female sexuality. Particularly, prophets Isaiah and Jeremiah prophesied against the perverted practices in the context of worship life of the people. They condemned what is known as the Fertility Cult associated with the Queen of Heaven, Child Sacrifices and the Festival of the Dead (See, Isaiah 57 and 56; Jeremiah 44).[5]

All these practices bear a lot of pornographic significance and are therefore vehemently condemned. To be sure, in the religion of Israel, the criterion for deciding the sinfulness of these sexual acts was whether they were in accordance with the holiness of God. To discourage the proliferation of such promiscuous acts, the parties involved were to be stoned to death in order to purge Israel of such evil and its memory.

In the book of Leviticus, the Bible says,

> "None of you shall approach anyone ... to uncover his nakedness: I am the Lord... You shall not uncover the nakedness of a woman and her daughter, nor shall you take her son's daughter or her daughter's daughter, to uncover her nakedness. They are near of kin to her. It is

---

[4] See, T. Drorah Setel, "Prophets and Pornography: Female Sexual Imagery in Hosea" in Letty M. Russell, ed., *Feminist Interpretation of the Bible*, (Philadelphia: Westminster, 1985), p. 86. See also the section "Pornographic Objectification of Women" in Shivraj K. Mahendra, "A Feminist Study of Selected Texts in the Bible," (Unpublished paper, UTC, November 2010), p. 5.

[5] Particularly, Isaiah 57: 3-10, 65:2 and Jeremiah 44:5-19.

wickedness. Nor shall you take a woman as a rival to her sister, to uncover her nakedness while the other is alive. Also you shall not approach a woman to uncover her nakedness as long as she is in her customary impurity [menstruation period]. Moreover you shall not lie carnally with your neighbor's wife, to defile yourself with her. And you shall not let any of your descendants pass through the fire to Molech, nor shall you profane the name of your God: I am the Lord. You shall not lie with a male as with a woman. It is an abomination. Nor shall you mate with any animal, to defile yourself with it. Nor shall any woman stand before an animal to mate with it. It is perversion." (Leviticus 18:6-23 NKJV).

In the above passage the "uncovering" is clearly a pornographic act and is strictly forbidden. In all the relations described, woman is representative of all women. It is not to be taken that with some women "uncovering" might be permitted. There is no relation left out; there is no woman with whom one should engage in pornographic act. Again, not only men with women, but men with men, women with women and humans with animals are not supposed to engage in pornographic behavior or uncovering, for it is sexual immorality and strictly forbidden.

The New Testament. In the New Testament we read, "Every sin that a man does is outside the body, but he who commits sexual immorality sins against his own body" (1 Corinthians 6:18). The Lord Jesus Christ said, "You have heard that it was said, 'You shall not commit adultery' (Exodus 20:14, see also, Leviticus 20:10 and Deuteronomy 5:18). But I say to you that everyone who *looks at* a woman with lust has already committed *adultery* with her in his heart."[6]

Apostle Peter surely described lovers of pornography when he spoke of those who had "eyes full of adultery" (2 Peter 2:14). This phrase is, in the words of Robertson, a "vivid picture of a man who cannot see a woman without lascivious thoughts towards her."[7]

Apostle Paul says, "Be sure of this, that no fornicator or impure person, or one who is greedy (an idolater), has any inheritance in the kingdom of Christ and of God" (Ephesians 5:5). The Bible clearly mentioned that, "whoremongers and adulterers will be judged by God" (Hebrews 13:4). We also read that, "the faithless, the polluted, the murderers, the fornicators, the sorcerers, the idolaters, and all liars, will have their part in *the lake that burns with fire and sulfur,* that is, hell"(Revelation 21:8).

Some people try to argue that looking at the naked body is not bad, because God made it beautiful, and that Adam and Eve were naked in the garden without any problem. But, that was before sin entered the scene. It is said that *the eye is the window of the soul.* What we stare at definitely affects us spiritually and can cause us to sin.[8] The sin takes place even before the action is executed. The Lord Jesus says in Mathew 5:28,

> "But I say to you that everyone who looks at a woman with lust has already committed adultery with her in his heart."

---

[6] Matthew 5:27-28 (NRSV).

[7] A. T. Robertson, *Word Pictures in The New Testament, Vol. VI*, (New York: Harper, 1930), p. 167.

[8] David *saw* the woman naked, before he got ideas to sin with her. See, 2 Samuel 11:2-5. Emphasis mine.

The latest craze in the Internet pornography is *Hentai* or Cartoon Porn.[9] Some people try to justify viewing Hentai by saying, "it does not involve real people." They argue that the Bible never condemns "art" as being sinful, and that Hentai is just an art. To be sure, the difference between art and pornography is the difference between beauty and lust. In art the nakedness is intended to be a display of beauty and wonder. Pornography does no such thing. Its intent is to entice a person by arousing the person's lust. When people say that they view pornography as an art and that it is beautiful, then it is nothing but an attempt to justify sin. According to the Bible, the three primary divisions of sin are: the lust of the flesh, the lust of the eyes, and the pride of life.[10]

Pornography, whether cartoon-based or not, definitely causes us to lust after flesh. In viewing pornography lustful passions and thoughts are activated in the heart and mind. This is obviously sinful and clearly demonstrates that pornography is sinful. Thus the Bible condemns pornography without any reservation.[11]

A Biblical Theology of Human Sexuality

The attempt in this section is to reconstruct a biblical theology of human sexuality so as to respond to the issue of pornography theologically. Here we shall focus specifically on the nature of the human person and divine purpose of sexuality as described in the Bible.

---

[9] Hentai is the Japanese term for "perversion." It is cartoon-based pornography created primarily on "anime," a popular form of Japanese animation. Hentai is also known as "manga" or "doujin." Also, there are some video games as well as online games where one can play pornography.

[10] 1 John 2:16.

[11] Additional and latest information could be found at, http://www.christiandoctrine.net and http://www.padfield.com/ (Accessed 15 January 2006).

Nature of a Human Being

The reason for analyzing the nature of a human being has its significance in that our thoughts, ideas and activities grow out of our very nature. The English word *nature* comes from the Greek *phusis* which means "basic deposit of *stuff* with which an individual is created or born."[12] The biblical portrayal of the nature of man (*adam* – human being, male and female) is as follows:

Material Nature of Human Being. Man[13] was created "out of the dust of the ground." In the book of Genesis we read, "... the LORD God formed man from the dust of the ground, and breathed into his nostrils the breath of life; and the man became a living being. (Genesis 2:7 NRSV) thus his nature is material. Man is from the earth (*adamah* – ground, material) and God has declared material creation as *very good*. It is only after the fall of man that the material creation was cursed and that both the natural world and sinfully habituated human flesh now cause problem.[14]

Spiritual Nature of Human Being. God formed man out of the dust of the ground, but it was only when the breath (or spirit, Hebrew: *ruakh*) of life was breathed into him that he became a living soul (or animate being).[15] This personal, direct and unique in-breathing of God in man distinguishes human creation from other animate

---

[12] For a detailed analysis of the nature of man see, Jay E. Adams, *A Theology of Christian Counseling: More Than Redemption*, (Grand Rapids: Zondervan, 1979), pp. 98-138. In this section I have derived my insights largely from this particular work.

[13] The use of *man* in this whole section is inclusive of both male and female (human being) and the pronoun *he* or *his* also refers to *them*.

[14] Jay E. Adams, *A Theology of Christian Counseling: More Than Redemption*, (Grand Rapids: Zondervan, 1979), p. 106.

[15] See, John Murray, *Collected Writings, Vol II*, (Carlisle: Banner of Truth, 1978), p.8.

life, e.g., animals and birds, etc. Thus because of this in-breathing of God, man consists of a spiritual or divine nature as well.

Moral Nature of Human Being. God has created man in his own image and likeness. We read in the Bible:

> "Then God said, "Let us make humankind in our image, according to our likeness; and let them have dominion over the fish of the sea, and over the birds of the air, and over the cattle, and over all the wild animals of the earth, and over every creeping thing that creeps upon the earth." So God created humankind in his image, in the image of God he created them; male and female he created them. God blessed them, and God said to them, "Be fruitful and multiply, and fill the earth and subdue it; and have dominion over the fish of the sea and over the birds of the air and over every living thing that moves upon the earth." (Genesis 1:26-28 NRSV).

It is in this likeness to God that man is different from the animals and becomes an intelligent, morally responsible being. Man is supposed to renew God's likeness by putting on true righteousness, holiness and full knowledge[16] since it is these elements that constitute the *image and likeness* (moral and intellectual qualities) of God in man/human beings.

Social Nature of Human Being. Man was created for a relationship-living. He was not supposed to remain alone but maintain a fellowship with both God and his fellow beings.[17] This social nature of man involves the commitment of love for the neighbors and obedience to God. A unique example of man's social living is marriage.

---

[16] See, Ephesians 4:23,24; Colossians 3:10.
[17] Genesis 2:18; Matthew 19 and 1 Corinthians 7.

Working Nature of Human Being. Man was created with a working nature. The necessity for work, to be a creative and productive being, is the characteristic of his nature. Work is work when it is biblically proper and satisfyingly productive. Man is created to work in such a way that he brings glory to God, contributes maintenance to whole creation and satisfaction to him (Genesis 1:28).[18]

Pornography attacks the dignity of men and women created in the image of God. The nature that pornography portrays of the human being is animalistic, carnal and irrational. It defiles his material nature, neglects the spiritual nature, distorts the social nature, corrupts the moral nature and misuses the working nature of man. This is a clear refutation of the defenses of pornography which believe that pornography can help overcome various sexual problems and reduce sex crimes, for by its denial of human dignity and emphasis on obscenity and lawlessness; pornography fails to create healthy sexual relationships.[19]

Divine Purposes of Human Sexuality

From the Word of God we can derive the following four godly purposes of human sexuality:

To Establish Union. Sex is intended by God to form a spiritual-physical union *between* a husband and wife – "one flesh" that is not to be broken (Genesis 2:24-25; Matthew 19:4-6). Pornography promotes lust, an intense sexual desire preoccupied with self gratification and provides the basis for the sin of adultery, and it never

---

[18] Cf. Genesis 2:15 and Colossians 3:22-4:1.

[19] John H. Court, *Pornography: A Christian Critique*, (Illinois: InterVarsity Press, 1980), pp. 16-17, 44-48.

cares for the spiritual union and social relationship of the partners.[20]

To Provide Intimacy. It is intended to provide physical intimacy *within* the marital bond and this sexual intimacy is to result in a deep personal understanding and care between husband and wife (Genesis 4:1, 17, 19:8). Such intimate knowledge is undermined by pornography, which encourages and glorifies casual, recreational or commercial sexual encounters.

To Provide Mutual Pleasure. Sex is intended to provide mutual pleasure for husband and wife (Proverbs 5:18-19). Pornography undermines true enjoyment by removing love and respect from sexual relationships and by treating people – particularly women and children – as mere objects to be exploited for periodic gratification or enjoyment.

To Procreate Progeny. Sexual intercourse is intended for the special purpose of procreation (Malachi 2:15 and Genesis 1:28). Pornography does not intend procreation; it is only committed to exhibition, distortion and exploitation of sex.

We see God that has given the gift of sex to human beings with specific purposes. But because of sin in the world (Romans 3:23) sex has been misused and abused (Romans 1:24-25). Pornography distorts God's gift of sex, which should be shared only within the bonds of marriage

---

[20] Darren E. Sherkat and Christopher G. Ellison, "The Cognitive Structure of a Moral Crusade: Conservative Protestantism and Opposition to Pornography" *Social Forces* 75:3, March 1997, pp. 957-980. For similar opinions see, Stephen Arterburn and Jim Burns, *When Love is Not Enough: Parenting Through Tough Times,* (Colorado: Focus on the Family, 1992); Jerry Falwell, *The New American Family: The Rebirth of the American Dream,* (Dallas: Word, 1992); and Liz Minnick, "Pornography" *Home Life,* 1994, pp. 41-43.

(1 Corinthians 7:2-3). Scripture specifically condemns the practices that result from pornography such as sexual exposure, adultery, bestiality, homosexuality, incest and prostitution (see, Genesis 9:21-23; Leviticus 18:6-18, 20, 22, 23; 20:13 and Deuteronomy 23:17-18)[21] and thus clearly warns against any misuse of sex. Premarital and extramarital sex (sex before and outside of marital bond) is condemned (1 Corinthians 6:13-18; 1 Thessalonians 4:3). Even thoughts of sexual immorality (often fed by pornographic material) are condemned (Matthew 5:27-28).

Theology and Pornography

This section seeks to reflect on pornography with regard to our relationship with God, the concern of Salvation and feminist response on the issue.

> "Though debased, pornography is a theological statement. It says: There is no God who says I should limit my lust or channel my passion or give as well as get... Pornography is anti-woman and anti-child. It is anti-marriage and anti-permanence. Thus is is profoundly anti-civilization. Since civilization is social support to the dynamics of life, pornography is anti-life."
> – William Stanmeyer

Pornography and God

The nature of human beings and divine purposes of human sexuality described above are of much theological significance in relation to the issue of pornography. It is really important to know that in the act of sex, God paints for us a picture of our union with Christ at His return. But pornography mocks the first institution ordained by

---

[21] Read, Genesis 9:21-23; Leviticus 18:6-18, 20, 22, 23; 20:13 and Deuteronomy 23:17-18.

God (marriage between man and woman) and subverts the most sacred behavior on this side of heaven. As already said, human sexuality is a gift of God to personal dignity, to family love, and to the present and future of human society. Where human sexuality is honored, life is ennobled. Where it is dishonored by sexual abuse, life is degraded, marriage is mocked, and children are scorned in their birthrights.[22] We can see pornography is anti-woman, anti-man and anti-children as it portrays their degraded, narrow, and exploited stipulations. It is anti-sex as well since it distorts and misrepresents God's special gift to human beings. Thus it is anti-family and anti-society. Above all, pornography is anti-life and anti-God and utterly blasphemous because it stands for everything that is exactly opposite to the divine purposes mentioned in the Bible.

Pornography and Salvation

For understanding pornography and salvation, we need to go back to the biblical teachings concerning sexual behaviour. The Lord Jesus taught that lust in the heart is adultery (Matthew 5:28). And his apostles taught that those who die in the sin of adultery go to Hell (1 Corinthians 6:9,10; Galatians 5:19-21; Revelation 21:8; etc.). Therefore, if any person lusts in their heart and dies in that condition, he/she goes to Hell. One must repent of this adultery and be pure in heart "to see God" (Matthew 5:8). "To see God" means to reach up to God, to be with God; this is a clear indication of the result of salvation. Only those who are saved will have the privilege to see God. It is also written, "If you live according to the sinful nature, you will die; but if by the Spirit you put to death

---

[22] See, Paul J. Murphy, "Pornography, Promiscuity, Perversion" *Homiletic & Pastoral Review, Vol. 89, No. 3*, December 1988, p. 62.

the misdeeds of the body, you will live" (Romans 8:13). "For the grace of God that brings salvation has appeared to all men. It teaches us to say 'NO' to ungodliness and worldly passions, and to live self-controlled, upright and godly lives in this present age" (Titus 2:11,12). Whom the Son (Lord Jesus) sets free is free indeed (John 8:36). Thus salvation can be attained by turning away from the sin of pornography and by concurrently believing in the saving grace of God in and through Christ. It is only the "believer" that has salvation. Those that don't continue to believe will be condemned (John 3:18b; Revelation 21:8; John 15:6).[23]

The spiritual damage done by pornography is serious and greatly devastating. By no means does pornography qualify according to what the Bible says we must think about,

> "whatever is *true*, whatever is *noble*, whatever is *right*, whatever is *pure*, whatever is *lovely*, whatever is *admirable* - if anything is *excellent* or *praiseworthy* - think about such things." (Philippians 4:8).[24]

Pornography is not true, it is not noble, it is not right, it is not pure, it is not lovely, and it is not admirable. It is neither excellent nor praiseworthy. Pornography is addictive and destructive and leads to ever-increasing wickedness (Please see, 1 Corinthians 6:12; 2 Peter 2:19; Proverbs 6:25-28; Ezekiel 20:30; Ephesians 4:19 and Romans 6:19). Lusting after other people (whether real or imaginary) in our minds is sin and is offensive to God.

---

[23] To read on *Lust and Pornography*, log on to, http://www.evangelicaloutreach.org/ This website has great resources for all. You will fine very useful materials on dealing with pornography and sexual addictions, among other things. (Accessed on 28 May 2012).

[24] Emphasis mine.

Continual viewing of pornography demonstrates that a person has not experienced the saving grace of God (1 Corinthians 6:9 and Matthew 5:28).[25]

Pornography in the Feminist Concerns

The critical characteristic of pornography is not that it deals with sexual themes, but that it eroticizes violence, humiliation, degradation and other explicit forms of abuse. Since women are the most frequent victims of pornography, feminists, too, have debated how to respond to it.[26] The objection that much of pornography is demeaning to women surfaced early in the contemporary feminist movement, particularly in Kate Millett's 1970 book *Sexual Politics*, which analyzed some of Henry Miller's limited and negative portrayals of women. The anti-pornography fight gained its greatest momentum in 1975 with the appearance of "snuff" films in the U.S. claiming to depict the actual killing and dismembering of female actors during explicitly sexual scenes, these films highlighted the link between sex and violence that

---

[25] For biblical answers on various issues, log on to, http://www.gotquestions.org/ For a detailed treatment on biblical theology of human sexuality see, Stanely Grenz, *Sexual Ethics: A Biblical Perspective*, (Carlisle: Paternoster, 1990); Roger Sonnenberg, *Human Sexuality: A Christian Perspective*, (St. Louis, USA: Concordia Pub. House, 1998) and Paul M. Quay, *The Christian Meaning of Human Sexuality*, (San Francisco: Ignatius Press, 1985). For yet another perspective on pornography see, Richard Griffiths, *Art, Pornography and Human Value: A Christian Approach to Violence and Eroticism in the Media*, (Bramcote: Grove Books, 1975).

[26] Mary Ellen Ross, "Censorship or Education? Feminist Views on Pornography" at http://www.religion-online.org/ and http://www.christiancentury.org/ (Accessed: January 15, 2006). I am greatly indebted to the author for much of the information reproduced in this section. See also, D. Marty Lasley, "A Theology of Pornography: Is There Anything Wrong With Nudie Pictures?" at http://www.americanwasteland.com/ (Accessed: January 15, 2006).

frequently characterizes pornography. The anti-pornography movement that flourished in this climate reached its most stringent form when feminist activists Andrea Dworkin and Catherine MacKinnon drafted the Indianapolis Anti-Pornography Ordinance in 1984.

This ordinance defined pornography as anything that presents women as sexual objects, as enjoying pain, humiliation or rape, or as being physically harmed. It also identified pornography as material that depicts women in "scenarios of degradation, injury, abasement, or torture." Underlying the ordinance is the assumption that pornography plays an important role in causing rape and domestic violence, and therefore is not only demeaning but constitutes an overt physical threat to women.

The efforts of MacKinnon and Dworkin have helped feminists recognize the inadequacy of the "sexual arousal" definitions of pornography; they have made them aware of the profound misogyny in pornography, and revealed how extensive pornographic images are in our culture.

Feminists believe that to construct a precise and effective critique of pornography, we must have a clear idea of what we consider normative sexual expression. Social and religious understanding of erotic life is totally absent in the privatized world of pornography. A sound theology of the body must not only celebrate male and female physicality but also acknowledge that sexuality is meant to help unite individuals, and ultimately communities, assert the feminists. Social ethicist and feminist theologian Mary Pellauer finds pornography problematic not because it is sexually explicit, but because it portrays violence and domination in a sexual context. She believes that good theology calls us to celebrate healthy human sexuality. Good theology can be helpful in clarifying what is at stake in porn. No one who celebrates healthy sexuality among the many goods of God's creation can affirm pornography.[27]

SUMMARY

Our task in this chapter has been to explore a biblical and theological response to the issue of pornography. We have seen that pornography attacks the dignity of men and women created in the image of God. The nature that pornography portrays of human beings is animalistic, carnal and irrational. Theologically, pornography proves to be anti-woman, anti-man and anti-children as it portrays their degraded, narrow, and exploited stipulations and thus it is anti-family and anti-society. Pornography is also one of the genuine moral and ethical concerns of our time. And it is this concern that forms the contents of the next chapter.

> *Pornography is not true, it is not noble, it is not right, it is not pure, it is not lovely, and it is not admirable. It is neither excellent nor praiseworthy. Pornography is addictive and destructive and leads to ever-increasing wickedness.*

---

[27] Mary Pellauer, "Pornography: An Agenda for the Churches," at www.christiancentury.org/ (Accessed: January 15, 2006). See also, Marcella Maria Althaus-Reid, "A Woman's Right to Not Being Straight (El Derecho a no ser Derecha): On Theology, Church and Pornography" *Concilium*, Vol. 2, 2002, pp. 88-96. For "Church and Sex Throughout History" see, Letha Scanzoni, *Sex and the Single Eye*, (Grand Rapids: Zondervan, 1968), pp. 22-37. For a feminist defense of pornography see "Pornography and Ethics" at http://www.muslimphilosophy.com/ (Accessed: January 15, 2006; Revisited on 28 May 2012).

Chapter 4

Ethical Concerns and Reflections

> *When taken through a scrutiny of different ethical models or paradigms, pornography comes out to be a very undesirable enterprise. It fails to lead us to any good end of life that could be pursued with aspiration.*

Introduction

Pornography is a serious moral concern today. Moral judgments presume that there are certain claims upon and goals of our actions which we are supposed to pursue. Ethics helps us to critically examine the basis of these claims and goals. Etymologically the term "ethics" has its root in the Greek word *ethos*. The term "ethos" refers to the "customs" or "character which distinguishes a particular people." Traditionally, *ethics* has been used interchangeably with *morals*. The term *moral* comes from the Latin *mos*, which means "custom" or "way of life."[1] Both terms have been used to connote those duties and responsibilities which persons have with reference to right or wrong conduct or ultimate purpose of life. Ethics also helps us to identify and analyze the *values at stake* and to find out ways towards appropriate or satisfactory solutions. In this chapter our focus therefore is to take up the issue of pornography with serious moral concerns and attempt towards drawing out some Christian ethical reflections.

---

[1] For details see, Hunter P. Mabry, ed., *Christian Ethics: An Introductory Reader*, (Serampore: ITL/SSC, 1987), pp. 3-6; and M. Stephen, *Introducing Christian Ethics*, (Delhi: ISPCK, 2003), pp. 1-5.

Christian Ethics on Pornography

As already mentioned, pornography is one of the major moral and ethical problems facing the world-society today. It is therefore important to bring pornography under ethical scrutiny and see whether it is able to stand the test of moral concerns and ethical paradigms. We shall analyze the issue primarily from a Christian ethical perspective. To be sure, the task of Christian Ethics is to make a critical study of the moral life of the Christian community[2] with the aim of disclosing the basic pattern of thinking and doing what is faithful to its character as a community of persons before God. As systematic, critical reflection upon Christian moral life, Christian ethics does not claim to have pre-formulated answers to all moral problems, but rather to provide a perspective, an approach and a framework for dealing with such problems. Since many Christians are struggling with this problem, it is appropriate to make use of Christian ethics as a tool to critically reflect on the issue.

The science of Christian Ethics provides us with some ethical modes of discourses. These modes or models can be used in the form of paradigms for the critical evaluation of the intensions and implications of pornography. This chapter utilizes the following three classical paradigms of ethical discourses, namely, Deontological Ethics, Teleological Ethics and Responsibility-Relationality Ethics. The significance of these paradigms can be seen in that they are vital for guiding human conduct in all spheres of life. We shall now engage with the scrutiny of pornography under these modes of ethical reflections.

---

[2] Not exclusively Christian community though. Whenever needed, or called to do so, it is also obliged and committed to contribute to the needs of other communities as well.

Deontological Ethics and Pornography

Deontological Ethics is the ethics of *obligation* or *duty*.[3] This approach is concerned with questions regarding *what is right*. It holds that there are moral laws and imperatives[4] which all persons have a duty to obey. This ethics raises the question, *what law or laws is my duty to obey?* Religiously this approach asks, *what are the laws of God to be followed?* What is our *dharma?* It assumes that what are most needed are rules, principles and structures to guide and retain the behaviour of persons and groups.[5] While applying the deontological paradigm to evaluate pornography, we will be considering the following questions: *Is pornography right? Does it obey the law of God? Does it lead me to perform my dharma?* We shall begin with the concepts of right and wrong.

Right and Wrong. Whether some act or deed is right or wrong is determined by the socio-religious guidelines of behaviour in a given social context. The idea of right or wrong is also concerned with the idea of benefit or harm. If something has to be right it has to be beneficial but without being harmful. The problem with pornography is that it appears to be a right thing to a few, but it is considerably wrong for the majority, especially to those who are used as objects. To provide or gain whatever *pleasure* or *benefit* at the expense of someone else's *freedom* and *dignity* is not right. Pornography is based on

---

[3] "Deontology" comes from the Greek *deon*, meaning *that which is obligatory*. It is the Study of Moral Obligation. See, Atkinson, David J. and David H. Field, eds. *New Dictionary of Christian Ethics and Pastoral Theology* (Leicester: Inter-Varsity Press, 1995), p. 297.

[4] For example, the Decalogue (The Ten Commandments, Exodus 20:1-17), or constitutional provisions regarding fundamental rights, and fundamental duties.

[5] Hunter P. Mabry, ed., *Christian Ethics: An Introductory Reader*, (Serampore: ITL/SSC, 1987), p.8.

perversion, exploitation and falsification of sexuality and personality and accordingly it is not right.

Rules and Regulations. Rules and regulations are designed to maintain and promote common good. They regulate individual as well as group behaviours so that the welfare of the society is not at stake and that its moral and ethical fabric is maintained and strengthened. The purpose of the law is good to all and harm to none. Pornography functions against moral and ethical laws, which are essential for the wellbeing of the society. It is against the divine law of sexual conduct. God has designed human sexuality with specific purposes. These purposes are to be accomplished in the honorable human sexual behaviours. What pornography does is the total disregard and mockery of those divine purposes. Thus it does not obey the law of God.

Responsibility and Obedience. Why do we follow time tables? If we do not follow time tables we will not be able to achieve certain goals on appointed times. What is the reason for human obedience? It is the sense of duty or responsibility that helps a person to obey certain rules and regulations. The whole duty (*dharma*) of human being is to obey God. For the life that we have is his special gift to us. Life is to be enjoyed in a way that it promotes welfare for all and harm to none. A life of peace and joy is possible but only with the presence of rules and committed and responsible obedience to those rules. Even nature obeys God by functioning systematically in the way it is designed and programmed. We see that there is an order or rule everywhere. There is no existence without law or order. Anything against this order is chaotic. Pornography is anti-law.[6] It is not obedient to the law of

---

[6] See, Leviticus 18. See also, *Biblical Response to Pornography* and *Divine Purposes of Human Sexuality*, in the preceding chapter.

sexual conduct and thus it is irresponsible and wrong. It is anti-order and eventually leads to chaotic consequences, proving to be nothing but a total *adharma*, (disobedience or unrighteousness).

The deontological ethics, with its emphasis on law and duty, promotes traditional morality rooted in the law of God. This is a clear refutation of the defenses that try to use pornography as a vehicle to overthrow the so called old repressive culture, the coldness of anti-sexual philosophy of traditional morality.[7] To be sure, these arguments are based on rejection of sexuality as part of God's creation and tend to lead towards anarchy in sexual conduct and are consequently invalid.

Teleological Ethics and Pornography

Teleological Ethics is the ethics of *ambition, good* or *ends*.[8] This approach is concerned with questions regarding the highest *good* or final *goal* of life towards which persons should aim. It holds that there are certain goods or ends which are worthy of complete commitment and it seeks to throw light upon what these are, for example, the 'Kingdom of God', a classless society, or constitutional objectives of building a democratic state. This ethics raises the question, *what is the highest good or end of life which a person should seek to serve?* Religiously this approach asks, *for what ultimate purpose has God created us?* How can we obtain *moksha or* liberation/salvation? Teleological approach assumes that what is most needed is greater clarity regarding *the ultimate end of life* and *how it is to be*

---

[7] John H. Court, *Pornography: A Christian Critique*, (Illinois: InterVarsity Press, 1980), pp. 23-28, 56-67.

[8] For "teleology" see, Atkinson, David J. and David H. Field, eds. *New Dictionary of Christian Ethics and Pastoral Theology* (Leicester: Inter-Varsity Press, 1995), p. 835.

*attained.*⁹ While applying the teleological paradigm to evaluate pornography, we will be considering the following questions: *Is pornography good?* Or *is pornography beneficial? And, what is the ultimate goal of pornography?* We shall begin with the concepts of good and bad.

Good and Bad. What determines something to be good or bad are the socio-religious criteria of general welfare in a given context. The idea of good or bad is concerned particularly with the concept of benefit or harm. If something has to be good it has to be beneficial but without being harmful. The problem with pornography is that it appears to be good to a few people, but it is greatly harmful for the larger community. To provide or gain whatever *pleasure* or *benefit* at the expense of someone else's *freedom* and *dignity* is not good. Pornography is a social evil promoting perversion, falsification and misrepresentation of human sexuality. It has no good in its motive; it treats persons as mere objects and destroys their dignity. In fact, it is self-destructive to those who claim to benefit from it, by leading them into abusive and criminal activities.¹⁰ Pornography does not care for or do any good to anybody and thus it is bad.

Goal and End. The question that needs to be addressed here is *what is the final goal of pornography* or *can pornography lead to or be a good end in itself?* Pornography generally claims to be catering to the needs of people with various sexual problems. Thus the intended goal of pornography seems to be that of providing sexual arousal and stimulation. But this goal includes aspects of

---

⁹ Hunter P. Mabry, ed., *Christian Ethics: An Introductory Reader*, (Serampore: ITL/SSC, 1987), p.8.

¹⁰ Among others, the confession of a serial murderer Ted Bundy, mentioned elswhere is an outstanding example. See also, Sean Thomas, "Self Abuse" *The Spectator*, June 28, 2003.

commercial benefits as well. As we have already seen, pornography is a huge business today. And the focus of any business enterprise remains but profit, profit by whatever means possible. Economically, this clearly leads to exploitation in the context of production. The victims of pornographic exploitation range from women to children. The fate of the consumers is also at stake. They are lead from one step to the other. One of the first outcomes is masturbation, which gradually leads to frustration and then search for real *objects* to satisfy the fantasies created by watching pornography.[11] Misrepresentation of sexual act promotes perversion and disorder[12] which gradually causes dissatisfaction and inspires criminal attitudes making pornography destructive in all its dimensions. Thus, whatever the expressed or intended goals are, the ultimate end of pornography is critically harmful for the society at large.

Glory and Shame. God has created sexuality with purpose and dignity. Sex is an integral part of the personality of the human being. This personality is essentially moral and significantly ethical. One of the concerns of the teleological paradigm is concept and act of *moksh* or salvation of human person, the total human personality. Salvation is a glorious enterprise of God to reconcile humanity to him. By living with faith in and obedience to Christ we have the privilege to receive the gift of God's glorious salvation. At the same time, by our disobedience resulted through faithlessness, we are

---

[11] Several examples can be found in the article "The Link Between Pornography and Violent Sex Crimes" by Robert Peters, President of Morality in Media, at http://www.moralityinmedia.org/

[12] See, Stein, Dan J., et.al., "Hypersexual Disorder and Preoccupation with Internet Pornography" *The American Journal of Psychiatry Vol. 158 (10)* October 2001, pp. 1590-1594. This article can also be read at http://gateway1.uk.ovid.com/ovidweb.cgi/

vulnerable to bring shame of condemnation upon ourselves. Persons involved in pornography have lost the sense of the *body as the temple of God*.[13] The result of pornographic negligence of a theology of the body has resulted in the exploitation and misrepresentation of it. Pornography has the ability to translate the glory of salvation into the shame of condemnation. Consequently, it is anti-salvation and fails to lead us to any *good end* of life that could be pursued with aspiration.

The teleological ethics, with its emphasis on aspiration and goal, promotes what is good and beneficial for all. This is a clear refutation of the defenses that attempt to present alternatives to traditional morality, good, beneficial, and glory by replacing love with hate, good with bad, and by deforming what is beautiful and praising ugliness.[14]

Responsibility-Relationality Ethics and Pornography

The Responsibility-Relationality Ethics emphasizes on responsibility in the context of a network of relationships. The primary concern of this approach is what action is most *fitting* in a given context. This model highlights that we live in human communities characterized by a net of ongoing relationships. The chief concern of this model is that our moral actions be *responsible*.[15] This approach asks, *what is going on? To whom are we responding and responsible? To what relationship must we be faithful? How can human solidarity be enriched and enhanced?*[16] With these

---

[13] 1 Corinthians 3:16 and 6:19.

[14] John H. Court, *Pornography: A Christian Critique*, (Illinois: InterVarsity Press, 1980), pp.20-23, 54-56.

[15] – that is, that they be actions taken with an awareness of what is happening, a willingness to be accountable, a concern for faithfulness in relationships, and a commitment to strengthen human solidarity.

[16] Hunter P. Mabry, ed., *Christian Ethics: An Introductory Reader*, (Serampore: ITL/SSC, 1987), p.7.

concerns in our mind, we shall now reflect on pornography under the following points.

Relations and Relationships. All Human relationships are based on virtues of faithfulness and loyalty to each other with the sense of belonging to one another. The concept of faithfulness, key to relational fabric and success, is alien to pornography. Also, love, care and constant fellowship are the characteristics of relationships which are completely missing in pornography. Pornography is concerned only with the flesh, only with the sensations. It is faithful to business and exploitative relations alone. It has no concern for care or fellowship and thus has nothing to do with any relationship, familial or societal. Clearly, pornography is anti-relationship as it does not care for or respect any relationship.[17] It destroys relationships and has no concern and no value for intimacy – the key to emotional, physical and spiritual relationship, unity and fruitfulness.

Responsibility and Accountability. Pornography does not take any responsibility in the context of sexual behaviour. Individuals are considered to be responsible for their own involvement and performance. Also, there is no concern for accountability in relationships as there is no love or care. In fact pornography promotes infidelity and promiscuity. In the context of pornography there is no accountability for persons and no respect for their dignity as they are treated as mere objects of carnal

---

[17] Several disturbing testimonies of pornographic victims include father's sexual exploitation of his own daughters. For similar opinions see, Richard Griffiths, *Art, Pornography and Human Value: A Christian Approach to Violence and Eroticism in the Media,* (Bramcote: Grove Books, 1975), pp. 20-21. Majority of incest sins are the sad results of pornographic addiction. For examples, log on to, http://www.moralityinmedia.org/ and http://www.obscenity crimes.org/.

gratification and exploitation. What God desires and has been doing is to bring humanity in responsible relationships.

Solidarity and Harmony. By its destructive approach to relationships and a totally neglected sense of responsibility, pornography proves to be nothing but a grave danger to human solidarity. The concept of relationship and responsibility are the key to human solidarity. Pornography breaks up the web of harmonization in human familial and social relational contexts. It is anti-relationship, anti-responsibility and consequently anti-solidarity.

The Responsibility-Relationality Ethics, with its emphasis on responsibility in the context of a network of relationships, promotes virtues of faithfulness and loyalty to each other. The concept of faithfulness is alien to pornography. This is a clear refutation of the defenses that favour pornography as part of the issue of freedom of speech,[18] for these defenders have failed to create a truly free society precisely because freedom for a few eventually becomes oppression for many. The lack of concern for others and lack of honesty or faithfulness in a relational context make the freedom of some people oppression for the others.

When taken through a scrutiny of different ethical models or paradigms, such as the above, pornography comes out to be a very undesirable enterprise. This is so because of the fact that it is evaluated primarily on the basis of a biblical-ethical framework and pastoral concerns of this book. But this does not mean that this kind of an evaluation is invalid, because the paradigms used in this

---

[18] John H. Court, *Pornography: A Christian Critique*, (Illinois: InterVarsity Press, 1980), pp. 28-29, 69-79.

chapter have taken into proper consideration the intensions and implications of pornography for the global society.

The Ethics of the Pornographer

Pornography is a market-driven industry aimed on making as much money as possible by whatever means possible. This industry is not about the ethical values of altruism, generosity, gentleness or liberty.[19] It is nothing but another form of prostitution. The pornographer usually has commercial motives, but these are best served in making the audience addicted.[20] In all that he or she does, the pornographer is an exploiter, profane, trickster and totally unethical.

Summary

In this chapter we have taken pornography through a serious scrutiny of different ethical models. We find the exploitative intensions and anti-social implications of pornography to be really dangerous for the society at large. But unfortunately both the production and the consumption of pornographic materials continue to grow Hence, it appears to be a serious problem, demanding genuine pastoral attention. Our next and final chapter, therefore, shall focus on dealing with pornography in a practical way.

> *Pornography is a market-driven industry aimed on making as much money as possible by whatever means possible. This industry is not about the ethical values of altruism, generosity, gentleness or liberty.*

---

[19] Alice Swann, "The Role of Pornographic Industry in the Destruction of Intimacy" in Lyndon Bowring, ed., *Searching for Intimacy*, (Bletchle, UK: Authentic Media, 2005), p. 4.

[20] Richard Griffiths, *Art, Pornography and Human Value: A Christian Approach to Violence and Eroticism in the Media*, (Bramcote: Grove Books, 1975), p. 19. For a detail on what "Tricks Pornographers Play" log on to *http://internet-filter-review.toptenreviews.com/tricks-pornographers-play.html/* (Accessed: January 15, 2006; Reaccessed on 28 May 2012).

Chapter 5

From Bondage to Freedom

> *To be sure, there is no problem that cannot be solved. There is hope for all. David, Mary of Egypt, Augustine of Hippo, Charles de Foucauld, Mike Cleveland and many other 'sinners and prostitutes' were able to turn from disordered sexual lives...*

Introduction

Getting introduced with the issue, being aware of its challenges and analyzing it from different perspectives are the prerequisites for dealing with any problem in a practical way. That is precisely what we have been doing with the issue of pornography in the previous chapters. The attempt of the current chapter is to suggest possible practical ways and means, by which we can stand against pornography, discard its desirability and get liberated from the bondage of pornographic addiction. We shall begin with a note on the use of pornography followed by a section on addiction and effects.

The Use of Pornography

Why have people been drowning into pornography? Several reasons form the answer to this question. Pornography uses the strong visual senses of men to promote lust and sensuality and thus it is attractive to many people. Pornography seems particularly attractive to those who are:

(1) Curious and or exploring about sex and sexuality,

(2) Feel that they have a high sex drive,

(3) Coping with stress and peer pressure,

(4) Lonely and or Depressed,

(5) Fearful of relationship and intimacy,

(6) Feeling of low self-worth and believing no-one will love them,

(7) Needing to escape reality or are Ignorant of reality,

(8) Single and celibate – pornography seems to be a better option than having a sexual relationship,

(9) Having unsatisfactory sexual experiences and think that this will help them find stimulation or remove pressure from their spouse if used as a source of personal stimulation, and

(10) Slaves of pornographic addiction, those who think they cannot live without it![1]

Addiction and Effects of Pornography

Pornography will take you farther than you want to go, keep you longer than you want to stay, and cost you more than you want to pay. – Mike Cleveland.

Addiction to Pornography

Psychologists have identified a five-step pattern in pornographic addiction.[2] Those steps are as follows:

---

[1] Some informations of this section are gratefully reproduced from http://www.care.org.uk/group/group.aspx?id=17169/ (Accessed: January 15, 2006).

[2] Another documentation on the topic is found in Victor Cline, *Where Do You Draw the Line?* (Utah: Brigham Young University Press, 1974).

Exposure. The first step in pornographic addiction is exposure or contact. Addicts have been exposed to pornography in many ways, ranging from sexual abuse to looking at widely available pornographic materials: magazines, videos or Internet.

Obsession. The second step is obsession or fixation which is an outcome of one's regular exposure to pornography. Persons who are repeatedly exposed to pornography, "keep coming back for more and more" in order to get new sexual towering. James L. McCough, of the University of California at Irvine, said that "Experiences at times of emotional or sexual arousal get locked in the brain by the chemical epinephrine and become virtually impossible to erase."[3] Thus it becomes an obsession or habit to keep watching pornography.

Escalation. At this stage previous sexual highs become difficult to attain. Therefore persons begin to look for presentations of more exotic forms of sexual behavior (hard core pornography) to bring them stimulation.

Desensitization. A fourth step in pornographic addiction is desensitization or a kind of loss of sensation. At this level, what was initially shocking becomes routine. Outrageous and disgusting sexual behavior is no longer avoided but sought out for more intense stimulation. Concern about pain gets lost in the pursuit of the next sexual experience.

Action. The fifth and final step in the pornographic addiction is action ("acting out the fantasies") or practice. Persons find pleasure in doing what they have seen. Every pornography addict does not become a serial murderer, a

---

[3] Kenneth Kantzer, "The Power of Porn" in *Christianity Today*, February 7, 1986, p. 18 as quoted in J. Kerby Anderson, ed. *Living Ethically in the 90s* (Illinois: Victor Books, 1990) p. 70.

child molester, or a rapist. However, many of them do look for ways to act out their sexual fantasies stimulated by the pornographic craving. And in the process, finally end up in destructive and criminal behaviours.

Effects of Pornography

The adverse effects of pornography range from psychological harm (shame, nightmares, fear, suicidal tendencies) to physical harm (rape,[4] torture, murder, sexually transmitted diseases). Thus, the effects of pornography can be generally classified under two but interrelated categories: psychological and sociological.

Psychological Effects. Research findings by Dr. James L. McGaugh at the University of California in Irvin shows that sexual arousal through the use of pornographic images has proven psychological effect.[5] It is seen that a person's memories of sexually arousing experiences get locked in the brain by chemical epinephrine. Once there, the memories are difficult to forget. This becomes a psychological problem with social consequences. Psychologist Edward Donnerstein of the University of Wisconsin found that exposure to pornography can lead to anti-social attitudes and behaviour. Men viewers tend to be more aggressive towards women, less responsive to pain and suffering of rape victims, and more willing to accept various myths about rape.[6] Pornography desensitizes persons to rape as a criminal offence.

---

[4] Read the news by Arvin Vincent, "Rape City Gets Inspiration From Rape Porn" *Hindustan Times*, Tuesday, September 27, 2005.

[5] Gary S Greig, *Issues From the Edge*, (California: Gospel Light, 1991), pp. 67-68.

[6] Edward Donnerstein, "Pornography and Violence Against Women" *Annal of the New York Academy of Science* 347 (1980), pp. 277-288 as mentioned in J. Kerby Anderson, ed. *Living Ethically in the 90s* (Illinois: Victor Books, 1990) p. 69.

Researchers Dolf Zillman and Jennings Bryant[7] showed that continued exposure to pornography had serious adverse effects on beliefs about sexuality in general and on attitudes towards women in particular. These researchers also found that massive exposure to pornography encourages a desire for increasingly deviant materials which involve violence, including sadomasochism[8] and rape. Sadomasochism is a psychosexual disorder in which erotic release is achieved through having pain inflicted on oneself. The term derives from the name of Chevalier Leopold von Sacher-Masoch, an Austrian who wrote extensively about the satisfaction he gained by being beaten and subjugated. The term is frequently used in a looser social context in which masochism is defined as the behaviour of one who seeks out and enjoys situations of humiliation or abuse. The association of pain with sexual pleasure takes the form of both masochism and sadism, the obtaining of sexual pleasure through inflicting pain on others. Often, an individual will alternate roles, becoming aroused through the experience of pain in one instance and through the infliction of pain in another. It is said that "pornography is the theory and rape is the practice."[9]

Diana Russell, a feminist author, notes the correlation between deviant behaviour (including abuse) and

---

[7] Dolf Zillman and Jennings Bryant, "Pornography, Sexual Callousness, and the Trivialization of Rape," *Journal of Communication* 32 (1982), pp. 10-21; also, Zillman, Bryant, Carveth, "The Effect of Erotica Featuring Sadomasochism and Beastiality on Motivated Inter-Male Aggression," *Personality and Social Psychology Bulletin* 7 (1981), pp. 153-159.

[8] *Encyclopedia Britannica 2004 Ultimate Reference Suite CD*, Encyclopedia Britannica, Inc.).

[9] Robin Morgan, as quoted in *Cassell's Dictionary of Sex Quotations*, (London: Market House Books, 1993), p. 188.

pornography. She also found that pornography leads men and women to experience conflict, suffering, and sexual dissatisfaction.[10] Also, we can see from a psychological point of view that pornography is anti-conscience for it is inimical to the psychological and moral developments of the human personality causing serious loss of sensitivity to discriminative use of sex, sexual abuse and real violence.

Sociological Effects. A recurrent argument from civil libertarians and defenders of pornography is that it does not have any social effects. In fact some argue that pornography can contain a therapeutic effect on society.[11] Nevertheless, there are a number of compelling statistics that suggest that pornography does have profound social consequences.[12] Statistical studies by sociologists Murray Straus and Larry Baron, University of New Hampshire, found that rape rates are highest in states that have high sales of sex magazines and lax enforcement of pornography laws. Family breakdown, and tension and conflict in close relationships are just two of the many harmful social consequences of pornography addiction. In addition, pornography consumption is one of the most common profile characteristics of rapists and serial murderers. An outstanding example of this case is Ted Bundy, a convicted serial killer and rapist, who testifies,

---

[10] Diana Russell, *Rape and Marriage* (1982), as quoted in J. Kerby Anderson, ed. *Living Ethically in the 90s* (Illinois: Victor Books, 1990), p. 69.

[11] John H. Court in his notable work, *Pornography: A Christian Critique* (Illinois: InterVarsity Press, 1980), examines and evaluates the case for pornography by analyzing various arguments. We have summarized these arguments in the beginning of Chapter 2.

[12] For additional examples log on to http://www.obscenitycrimes.org/ (Accessed 15 January 2006).

> "I have lived a long time in prison now. And I've met a lot of men who were motivated to commit violence just like me. And without exception every one of them was deeply involved in pornography."[13]

Yet another outstanding example is Arthur Gary Bishop, convicted of sexually abusing and killing five young boys. He said,

> "If pornographic material would have been unavailable to me in my early states, it is most probable that my sexual activities would not have escalated to the degree they did... I am a homosexual pedophile convicted of murder, and pornography was a determining factor in my downfall."[14]

This is a clear refutation of the Evidence Argument,[15] which says pornography has no effect upon a person's character and that it is not harmful.[16] To be sure, the Evidence Argument is based on insufficient research, distortion of facts, and devoid of moral concerns, making the argument significantly invalid.

Pornography leaves the impression that sex has no relationship to privacy, that it is unrelated to love,

---

[13] Interview with Ted Bundy by James Dobson, 25 January 1989, as quoted by Trevor Stammers "The Web of Pornography" in Lyndon Bowring, ed., *Searching for Intimacy*, (Bletchley, UK: Authentic Media, 2005), p. 21.

[14] Information retrived from http://www.probe.org/ (Accessed on 15 January 2012).

[15] The American *Presidential Commission Report on Obscenity and Pornography, 1970*. See, John H. Court, *Pornography: A Christian Critique*, (Illinois: InterVarsity Press, 1980), pp. 13-16. This report was based on insufficient research and misinterpretation of facts.

[16] John H. Court, *Pornography: A Christian Critique*, (Illinois: Inter Varsity Press, 1980), pp. 30-43.

commitment, or marriage, that perverted forms of sexual activity are the most gratifying, that sex with animals is desirable, and that there are no adverse consequences – no venereal disease, divorces, or moral decay.[17]

Several decades ago Professor J. D. Unwin of Cambridge carried out a study on the sexual practices of more than 80 primitive and more advanced societies. He concluded that sexually permissive behavior led to less cultural energy, less creativity, less individualism, less mental development, and less cultural progress in general. Primitive societies with the greatest sexual freedom made the least cultural advances.[18]

Philosophically speaking, pornography simultaneously subjectifies men and masculinity and masculinises subjectivity (agency, will, desire, speech, sight) and objectifies women (silences, passifies, and frames women) and feminises objectivity; separating thereby Subject from Object (Man from Woman), Mind from Body (Masculine from Feminine) and the Eye/I of the beholder from the observable world he speaks and sees and offers up as object for the collective pleasure and perusal of other similarly positioned subjects.[19]

Spiritually speaking, pornography darkens our understanding and separates us from the godly life. Mike Cleveland testifies,

> "... when I was doing pornography and masturbation I was separated from God and God did not hear my prayers. In fact, my constant

---

[17] David Hocking, *The Moral Catastrophe*, (Oregon: Harvest House Publishers, 1990), p. 118.

[18] David Hocking, *The Moral Catastrophe*, (Oregon: Harvest House Publishers, 1990), p. 118.

[19] Geraldine F., "Nobodies Speaking: Subjectivity, Sex, and the Pornography Effect," *Philosophy Today*, Summer 1989, p. 178.

sinning caused Him to hide His face from me... I felt as if my prayers stopped at the ceiling and then fell to the floor. Even though I may have been a Christian I was "darkened in my understanding and separated from the life of God..." (Ephesians 4:18). Indeed, this was a very dark time in my life..."[20]

From a cultural perspective pornography proves to be anti-culture as it presents a distorted and false view of the world. It is also anti-community because it promotes crimes and corruptions in the given community.

From an ecological perspective pornography is anti-environment also as it is polluting our environment through visual garbage. Seriously enough, as an annihilistic reductionist and destructive evil pornography is anti-life.

In simple terms, watching pornography affects the whole person – physically, mentally, emotionally, and spiritually. No one can be immune to its corrupting effects. Pornography debases sexuality, corrodes human relationships, exploits women, youth and children, undermines marriage and family life, destroys ministries, fosters anti-social behavior, and weakens the moral fabric of the society.[21] It also opens the way for demonic attack and intrusions.

To Those who are in Bondage

Whatever be the reasons for pornographic consumption or addiction, it is extremely important to be aware that this is not beneficial in any sense and that it is really harmful in every sense. Some people, who have got

---

[20] Mike Cleveland, *Setting Captives Free: Pure Freedom, Breaking the Addiction to Pornography*, (Minnesota: Focus Publishing, 2002), p.11.

[21] Varughese Philip, "Pornographic De-Addiction: A Pastoral Approach," *Revive*, July 2010, p. 15.

entangled into the trap of pornography and want to get out of it, think that there is no way out! This is not true. To be sure, there is no problem that cannot be solved. There is hope for all. What we essentially need is a will to be freed. To be sure, there is no problem that cannot be solved. There is hope for all. David, Mary of Egypt, Augustine of Hippo, Charles de Foucauld, Mike Cleveland, Sean Thomas and many other 'sinners and prostitutes' were able to turn from disordered sexual lives to creative submission to God.[22]

The Single Persons

Three things are very important for the single persons to remember in relation to sex: Right Time, Right Purpose and Right Value. There is a time for everything (Read, Ecclessiastes 3). Everything has a value and a purpose. Pornography is promoting sexual activities without any restriction of age or time. It does not give the due value to sex and sexual relationship. It presents sex as an item of performance. It works against the divine purpose of sexuality. It is vital for the single persons to know that anything before its time will only bring disorder in life and hindrance on the way to success. The need is to focus on what is most important, and wait for the right time to enjoy the gift of sex in a right way and in a right context.[23]

---

[22] See, Anne Bayley, *One New Humanity: The Challenges of AIDS*, (London: SPCK, 1996 and Delhi: ISPCK,1998 reprint 2005), p. 200. For Sean Thomas' story see, "Self Abuse," *The Spectator*, 28 June 2003, pp. 16-18.

[23] For information on premarital sexual behaviours and sex and single persons, see, Anthony Grugni, *Sex Education*, (Mumbai: St. Pauls, 2002), Lewis B. Smedes, *Sex for Christians: The Limits and Liberties of Sexual Living*, (Grand Rapids: William B. Eerdmans Pub. Co., 1976, reprint 1981), Jason Perry, *How Far Can You Go?* (Mumbai: GLS

Another important thing to be remembered is the concept of real and false. Most single persons live in a world of fantasy. This fantasy world is further beautified in the pornographic works. Extremely beautiful girls with perfect bodies and greatly desirable appearances are the main contents in pornography. But reality is far from fantasy. We need to distinguish between what is real and what is false. The beauty that pornography portrays is false but the abhorrence that is observed is real. It is through a serious reflection on the negative impact of pornography on personality, career and future that we will be able to resolve to get rid of this destructive and exploitative evil.

The Married Persons

According to the India Today 2011 Sex Survey, 66% of the husbands are addicted to porn.[24] Married persons addicted to pornography have lost their way in the world of sexual passion. It is the distorted view of sexuality and diverted focus from true relationship with one's spouse that have caused this problem. Married persons need to know three things in relation to sex: The Purpose, The Value and The Purity. The awareness of the divine purpose of sexuality is essential for a happy married life. The value of sex has to be discovered within the bonds of marital relationship. It is important that the purity of sex, as a gift of God for unity, pleasure and procreation, be maintained among the couples. The focus of the married persons needs to be on strengthening their sexual relationship by mutual rediscovery of each other's liking and disliking. Any biased approach to satisfaction will

---

Publishing, 2004), and Ravi Zacharias, *Sense and Sensuality*, (Chennai: RZIM Life Focus Society, 2003).

[24] *India Today*, December 5, 2011, pp. 1 and 45.

only disturb the family and lead it to breakups. Commitment for accountability to one's spouse is the best way to keep from alluring options. Also, spiritual and emotional satisfaction, the key to healthy companionship, is greater than the physical.

Married persons also need to know that there is a difference between the real people and pictorial or celluloid ideals. Pornographic presentation portrays seemingly beautiful women with perfect physical structure and really sought-after look, motivating the person to dislike one's spouse. The need is to distinguish between what is real and what is false. The beauty portrayed by pornography is not real but artificial. It is not relational but commercial, thus it is not emotional but mere physical. We need to seriously reflect upon the negative consequences of pornography on family and society so that we will be able to resolve to get rid of this vicious and abusive evil.[25]

To those who are in bondage of pornography, whether single or married, there is hope of deliverance. There are several practical suggestions and steps to be followed in the struggle to be liberated. These steps are dealt under Pastoral Care and Pornography below. But let me also talk to those who are free!

---

[25] Suggested readings on this section include, Tim LaHaye, *The Act of Marriage*, (Secunderabad: OM Books, 2004), George Kaitholil, *Marriage Call to Holiness*, (Mumbai: St Pauls, 2000), Margaret Gill, *Free to Love: Sexuality and Pastoral Care*, (Secunderabad: OM Books, 2004), Douglas A. Anderson, *New Approaches to Family Pastoral Care*, (Philadelphia: Fortress Press, 1980), and Pater Lane, *Setting the Captives Free* (Milton, Australia: Exodus Asia Pacific, 2005). See also, Pastoral Theology of Sex and Marriage by Reuel L. Howe, in Doniger, Simon, ed., *Sex and Religion Today*, (New York: Association Press, 1953). Another recent and interesting book is Dale S. Kuehne's *Sex and the iWorld: Rethinking Relationship beyond an Age of Individualism*, (Grand Rapids: Bake Academic, 2009).

To those who are Free

It should not surprise us that there are people who have not even heard about pornography. Many of them have never been exposed to it and are unaware of its dangers. These people seem to be free from pornographic exposure and addiction. But they cannot be categorized as permanently safe persons. They are vulnerable to the exposure and consumption of pornography day by day. They need to be careful to avoid every possible contact or exposure to this evil. Apart from a real commitment to remain unaffected by pornography these people can have a passion to help those that are affected and struggling. Persons as well as groups can make positive contributions in dealing with the problem of pornography in many ways.

As Responsible Individuals

It is not enough to be self-protective and remain personally free from any addiction to pornography. As responsible citizens and individuals we must be willing to help our peers, colleagues and other fellow-individuals to come out of it and not to fall into its trap. We need to care for others' welfare and show responsibility in dealing with issues facing individuals around us today. This calls for the boldness to talk about the issue and engage with people in need of help.

As Parents and Families

As parents and families we have got the privilege and responsibility to raise responsible citizens who will contribute to the moral and ethical strength of our family and society. We have a role to play and an opportunity to teach the new generation with practical examples of living a life of sexual purity. It is observed that,

> In the absence of social interaction and parental guidance on sex, children are likely to turn to the Internet. Parental supervision of Internet access by the young is still not done on a widespread scale in India. As a result, pornography sites are rampantly accessed.[26]

We must redouble our efforts to provide sound moral formation to our children and youth. We must talk to our children about right sexual behaviours and instruct them in the biblical theology of human sexuality.

As Church and Institutions

Church and institutions, as divine organs of care and order in the contexts of everyday interactions, are responsible to provide clear teaching of the faith and objective moral truth, including the truth about sexual morality. To provide atmosphere and opportunity for all to learn and reflect on issues, such as pornography, facing our church and society, therefore, must be among the chief concerns of the Church and institutions today. In an age of permissiveness and moral confusion the Church needs to be a prophetic voice. Church sermons must occasionally focus on issues such as pornography and institutions must organize seminars and forums on such issues.

Christians in general must do the following things. First, they must work to keep themselves pure by fleeing immorality (1 Cor. 6:18) and thinking on those things that are pure (Phil. 4:8). As a man thinks in his heart, so is he (Prov. 23:7). Christians must make no provision for the flesh (Rom. 13:14). Pornography fuels the sexual desire in abnormal ways and can eventually lead to even more

---

[26] Chaitanya Karehalli, "Young and Kinky," *India Today*, December 5, 2011, p. 68.

debased perversions. We must, therefore, "abstain from fleshly lusts which war against the soul" (1 Peter 2:11). Second, Christians must work to remove this sexual perversion of pornography from society.

Pastoral Care and Pornography

Pornography is a serious concern of and challenge for the ministry of pastoral care and counseling today. In this section we shall see some pastoral steps and approaches in dealing with the issue of pornography. Philip suggests that,

> "Church as a healing community and pastor as a soul-carer has a great responsibility to address the issue of pornography. Biblical conviction, spiritual development, moral development, and environmental transformation play vital roles in overcoming pornographic tendencies."[27]

We shall begin with the role of the pastor.

Pastor as Helper

Pastor as a counselor and helper has a great role to play in helping people, especially of his or her congregation, to protect themselves and or to be freed from the clutches of pornography. The pastoral call to care for the needs of the congregation on various family and social issues is a significant call. Pastor is responsible to see that his or her congregation is made aware of the sexual problems in the society and help them face these problems using biblical paradigms. In his role as a helper, the pastor's success depends much on his own personal strength of character. The sense of self-redemption and a passion to help others are the keys to pastoral ministry.

---

[27] Varughese Philip, "Pornographic De-Addiction: A Pastoral Approach," *Revive*, July 2010, p. 15.

Identifying a Porn Victim

In order to help people get rid of pornography first of all we need to identify the victim. To do this it is not enough to have a general interest in people, what we need as pastors is a genuine concern that cares for *what is going on*. This is a relational challenge for a pastoral watch on the walk of the people. Also, mere identification is not sufficient. The awareness of someone's pornographic addiction must lead us to serious efforts to deal with it. Preaching has to be accompanied by practice; this is a challenge for walking the talk.

Counseling a Porn Victim

Counseling a porn victim is a special challenge. At least three factors need to be kept in mind while engaging with people struggling with pornography. First of all, genuine sensitivity to the feelings of the counselee has to be maintained. Attitude of criticism and or humiliation on the part of the counselor will never be helpful. Criticism and humiliation must be avoided. Secondly, true respect for the counselee as a person is important. It is the personality of the victim that is to be influenced for a commitment to purity-living. Finally, a friendly and tolerant attitude will be more effective to strengthen the effort in helping the porn addict. Also, in counseling a porn victim the use of spiritual resources (such as, scripture, prayer and sacraments) will be of tremendous help and influence.

Rehabilitation of a Porn Victim

The key to rehabilitation is to provide hope and trust to the person under care. At least three factors need to be kept in mind while working on the rehabilitation of a porn addict. First, the addict has to be accepted as a person, not as an object or case. Secondly, patience throughout the time of rehabilitation is essential. The slow progress in improvement may cause frustration, but this has to be dealt with determination, hope and trust. Finally, constant fellowship and needed appreciation will boost the progress. The hope to get freed and trust in the saving power of God working through the counselor will fasten the process of rehabilitation of a porn victim.

Breaking the Porn Addiction

Dealing with pornographic addiction is a great challenge. It requires conscious effort. It demands practical hard work and discipline. Several steps have been suggested towards freedom from the bondage of pornography.[28] The best and most effective way appears to be the religious or spiritual way. The Select seven-steps[29] to break the stronghold of pornography are as follows:

Step 1: Realize the Problem. Realize the destructive consequences of pornography and grasp the seriousness of your sin. Realize that you have a problem and that you need to deal with the problem. Have the right view and value of sex and sexuality. Go back to the ethical

---

[28] For example, D. James Kennedy and Franklin Graham, "Ten Ways to Break the Stronghold of Pornography," *Forerunner*, June 2005; "Ten Steps To Freedom In Christ" at, http://www.cbn.com/ spirituallife/ CBNTeachingSheets/ Pornography.asp (Accessed: January 15, 2006). Two of the best books on strategies for victory in the real world of sexual temptation are, Stephen Arterburn and Fred Stoeker with Mike Yorkey, *Every Young Man's Battle,* (Colorado: WaterBrook Press, 2004), Mike Cleveland's *Pure Freedom: Breaking the Addiction to Pornography,* (Minnesota: Focus Publishing, 2002), and Stephen Arterburn and Fred Stoeker with Mike Yorkey, *Every Man's Battle: Winning the War on Sexual Temptation One Victory at a Time,* (Colorado: WaterBrook Press), This book also contains sections written especially for the wives of men who struggle with pornography.

[29] Reformulated by the present author, these steps are based on the suggestions of several experts and specialists.

evaluation of the issue in this book and think through it. Pornography is a sin. It has to be confessed. Confess it, and God is willing to forgive you.

> *If we confess our sins, he who is faithful and just will forgive us our sins and cleanse us from all unrighteousness. - 1 John 1:9*

Step 2: Realize your Personal Identity. Look at yourself. Who you are? A man or woman created in the image of God. A person created with dignity and gifted with wisdom. A person who can make a difference in the society with positive influence. You cannot be doing things which even the animals don't do. You cannot enjoy dirt and filth. You are a new creation in Christ, your identity is for making impact. You are created to make a history.

> *So if anyone is in Christ, there is a new creation: everything old has passed away; see, everything has become new! - 2 Corinthians 5:17*

Step 3: Practice the Presence of God. Realize the presence of God in all places at all times and turn to the Lord Jesus for forgiveness and grace. Don't do anything in private that you cannot do in public. God wants to save you and give you a new life. Realize the fact that you may not be able to receive salvation, if you remain addicted to porn. Cultivate the fear of God in yourself. Come to Jesus, He is able to Cleanse you through his redeeming blood. There is joy and peace in God's presence.

> *Instead, as he who called you is holy, be holy yourselves in all your conduct; for it is written, "You shall be holy, for I am holy." - 1 Peter 1:15-16*

> *Submit yourselves therefore to God. Resist the devil, and he will flee from you. Draw near to God, and he will draw near to you. Cleanse your hands, you sinners, and purify your hearts, you double-minded. - James 4:7-8*

Step 4: Be Careful and Conscious. Identify the opportunities, contexts and situations that motivate or influence you to draw into pornography and be careful to avoid them consciously. Avoid loneliness, be social, set a goal, find an ambition and keep yourself really busy. We have always known, "An empty mind is the devil's workshop." And do not forget, God is watching over us! His Spirit is everywhere.

> *Where can I go from your spirit? Or where can I flee from your presence? If I ascend to heaven, you are there; if I make my bed in Sheol, you are there. If I take the wings of the morning and settle at the farthest limits of the sea, even there your hand shall lead me, and your right hand shall hold me fast. - Psalm 139:7-10*

Step 5: Take Authority over Your Eyes. Do not look at anyone lustfully. Do not look back to pornographic advertisements, pictures and posters. Train your mind to take impure thoughts captive, and guard your heart with all diligence. Be resolved to do your utmost for what is good and beneficial for all and to discard what is bad and filthy. In life, there are better things to focus and strive for.

> *"I have made a covenant with my eyes; how then could I look upon a girl?" - Job 31:1*
>
> *"... looking to Jesus the pioneer and perfecter of our faith, who for the sake of the joy that was set before him endured the cross, disregarding its shame, and has taken his seat at the right hand of the throne of God."*
> *- Hebrews 12:2*

Step 6: Take Help from Others. If you feel you cannot do it alone, get help. Choose persons, friends, fellowships and ministries that can help you to discard pornography and make a difference. Have accountability partners (spouses and close friends will be the best at this) who will check your life on a regular basis. Do not hesitate to share your problem to the individuals and groups (pastors, friends or institutions) that are committed to help you to get rid of porn addiction and achieve liberation.

> *But one is tempted by one's own desire, being lured and enticed by it; then, when that desire has conceived, it gives birth to sin, and that sin, when it is fully grown, gives birth to death. Do not be deceived, my beloved. - James 1:14-16*

Step 7: Follow the principle of the Shift of Energy Focus. When tempted, do some physical exercise or some hard work (e.g., push-ups or sit-ups) till your mind is off *the thing*. You may also practice what is called *bounce the ball*. As soon as your eyes see any person or picture make sure that you do not gaze upon, just bounce your eyes! Look at something else, something different, such as trees or buildings! Remember Job's covenant with the eyes. Spend quality times with God, read the Bible (particularly, memorize the following scripture portions: James 1:14-15; 1 Corinthians 6:18-20 and Ephesians 6:10-18),[30] and pray regularly for victorious living.

> *Turn away from fornication! Every sin that a person commits is outside the body; but the fornicator sins against the body itself. Or do you not know that your body is a temple of the Holy Spirit within you, which*

---

[30] Other very helpful Bibles verses include: Genesis 39; Psalm 51, 119:9-11; Proverbs 6:20-24, 23:26-28; Daniel 3; and Matthew 26:41; Mark 7:20-23; Luke 4:1-12; John 10:10, 15:1-17, 17:3; Acts 15:28-29; Romans 1:16-32, 6:23, 7:15-8:14, 12:1-2, 13:12-14; 1 Corinthians 10:12-13; 2 Corinthians 10:3-5; Galatians 5:1, 13, 16-18; Ephesians 2:10, 5:1-33; Philippians 4:8; Colossians 3:1-10; 1 Thessalonians 4:1-; 1 Timothy 6:11-12; 2 Timothy 2:22; Titus 2:11-14; 1 Peter 2:16, 4:1-6; Hebrews 4:15-16; James 4:1-10; and Revelation 2:7.

> *you have from God, and that you are not your own? For you were bought with a price; therefore glorify God in your body.* - 1 Corinthians 6:18-20

The Shift of Energy Focus is a personal approach adopted by the author to deal with emotional fluctuations, critical situations and complicated issues. What is done in this principle is a temporary change of focus from one activity to the other, basically to refresh the mind and do the most fitting and good things in a better way in a given time and context. By constant practice, the temporary shift becomes permanent shift. That is, the practice helps to develop a habit of the mind to be ever creative, competitive and contributive in what is excellent for all.

Once we have made a resolution to turn away from the sin of pornography, we must practically follow these steps in order to achieve lasting triumph over pornographic temptation and addiction.

However, some obstacles must be mentioned which may greatly hinder the process of liberation. We need to be seriously conscious about the influences of drugs or alcohol, peer-groups and the very human nature! Any intoxicant will only make you prey to the temptation. Drinking etc. will only make you fall back, never help rise up. Do not do anything under the peer-pressure. Do not follow the crowd in doing wrong. Know that you are a weak human being. That there is a sin within you that naturally attracts you to evil. Repeat the steps. With God's grace and your constant practice you can overcome all the obstacles.

Towards a Common Response

Media persons and professional communicators need to formulate and apply moral principles and ethical codes for the communication media which respects for the common good and promotes sound human development. Internet missions need to be founded and more powerful websites with pure and creative contents need to be launched. Let gospel messages pop up like the advertisement pop ups on the Internet.

Educators and schools need to emphasize the urgency for the respect of the human person, the value of family life, and the importance of personal sexual integrity. Young people in particular need to stand against the tide of pornography and violence in the media by responding positively to their parents and educators and especially by taking responsibility for their own moral decisions in the choice of entertainment and pleasure.

The general public, especially the Christian believers, also needs to raise her voice against all forms of pornography. Legislators and law enforcement officers need to take the problem of pornography seriously. Appropriate and accurate laws must be enacted where they are lacking, weak laws have to be strengthened and existing laws must be enforced without any compromise.[31] With such joint efforts only the proliferation of this evil can be thwarted.

The Lordship Prayer

One of the best common responses will be to sincerely and passionately offer the following "Lordship Prayer"[32] and live our personal lives accordingly.

> Lord Jesus, I acknowledge my need of you and accept you as my Saviour, my Deliverer and my

---

[31] See, Karackat Francis, *The Mass Media from a Christian Perspective*, Bangalore: Kristu Jyoti Pub., 2001, p. 91; cf. Pontifical Council for Social Communications Media: A Pastoral Response, 1989.

[32] Distributed by Ray Eicher, Mussoorie. Used with oral permission. 23 June 2012.

> Lord. I invite you to be the Lord (the authority) in the whole of my life.
>
> Lord of my human spirit and all my spiritual awareness and worship.
>
> Lord of my mind, my attitudes, my thinking, my beliefs, and my imagination. Lord of my emotions, my expression, and my feelings. Lord of my will and my decisions.
>
> Lord of my body, my health, my diet, my exercise, my rest and my appearance. Lord of my sexuality and its expression.
>
> Lord of my family and all my relationships.
>
> Lord of my work.
>
> Lord of all things that I have, and all my needs.
>
> Lord of my finances.
>
> Lord of my plans, my ambitions and my future.
>
> Lord of my life and the timing of my physical death.
>
> Thank you that your blood was shed that I might be free from the punishment due for my sin and that my name is written in the book of life.
>
> Amen.

Finally, be strong in the Lord and in the strength of his power. Put on the whole armor of God, so that you may be able to stand against the wiles of the devil. For our struggle is not against enemies of blood and flesh, but against the rulers, against the authorities, against the cosmic powers of this present darkness, against the spiritual forces of evil in the heavenly places.

> *Therefore take up the whole armor of God, so that you may be able to withstand on that evil day, and having done everything, to stand firm. Stand therefore, and fasten the belt of truth around your waist, and put on the breastplate of righteousness. As shoes for your feet put on whatever will make you ready to proclaim the gospel of peace. With all of these, take the shield of faith, with which you will be able to quench all the flaming arrows of the evil one. Take the helmet of salvation, and the sword of the Spirit, which is the word of God. Pray in the Spirit at all times in every prayer and supplication. - Ephesians 6:10-18*

Summary

This chapter has made us aware of the process of addiction to and effects of pornography. Pornography has negative effects on the persons and society is very clear in the study. Then an attempt has been made to provide in outline select approaches in dealing with the problem of pornography in a practical way. As far as the seriousness of the problem is concerned, the content of this chapter is only tentative and suggestive. Pastors, professional counselors, clinical psychiatrists and other specialists will be able to suggest additional or more effective approaches from their own studies and experiences.

> *The end of sexual passion aroused by pornography is void and empty. It never gets fulfilled. It is nihilistic and endless emptiness.*

Conclusion

It is high time for us to make a difference by living a life of purity, integrity and responsibility in the context of a confused, perverted and permissive world. And in order to do this, we need to discard the false attractions of pornography, give up the willing slavery to this destructive evil and live a life of holiness as victorious people of a Holy God.

Towards conclusion, it will be appropriate to outline what we have been doing in the book as a whole. In the first chapter, we have dealt with the etymology and select definitions, origin and development and the appearance and availability of pornography. In the second chapter, we have focused on a general survey of the global phenomena, legal matters, the defenses of pornography, and the debate of the acceptability of pornography with special reference to the Indian context. These two chapters, including the introduction, have thus set the stage towards systematic responses to the issue in the subsequent chapters.

The first response to the issue of pornography, presented in the third chapter, is a biblical and theological response. Taking scriptural support from the Bible, this chapter has attempted to reconstruct a Christian theology of human sexuality. Pornography as a form of sexual immorality is considered to be more disgusting than any other sexual evil in the Bible. Both the Old Testament and the New Testament have strong resentment on the issue of sexual immorality. *Though the defenders of pornography continue to argue for its desirability and harmlessness, they constantly fail to prove their positions, as pornography in reality attacks the dignity of men and women created in the image of God, defiling their material nature, neglecting their spiritual nature, distorting their social nature, corrupting their moral nature and misusing their working nature.* Thus, from a biblical and theological point of view, it proves to be anti-God as it is opposed to the purpose and design of sexuality created by God and stands contrary to the teachings of the Lord Jesus Christ about purity and love.

A second response, attempted in the fourth chapter, is a moral and ethical reflection on the issue of pornography as a whole. Here, select ethical models have been used to critically evaluate the impact of pornography. The Deontological ethics, with its emphasis on law and duty, promotes traditional sexual morality rooted in the law of God, whereas pornography is anti-law. The Teleological ethics, with its emphasis on aspiration and goal, promotes what is good and beneficial for all, whereas pornography is opposed to all these concerns. The Responsibility-Relationality Ethics, with its emphasis on responsibility and accountability in the background of a network of relationships, promotes virtues of faithfulness and loyalty in the context of sexual conduct. These virtues are alien to pornography. *Though the supporters of pornography continue to argue for its usefulness and benefits, they constantly fail to prove their positions, as pornography when taken through a scrutiny of different ethical paradigms, comes out to be a very undesirable enterprise.* In the final analysis, therefore, pornography leads to complete destruction of the victim. Let us not forget that the end of sexual passion aroused by pornography is voide and empty. It never gets fulfilled. It is nihilistic and endless emptiness.

The third response to the issue of pornography, offered in the fifth and last chapter, is a pastoral response. Analyzing the process of addiction and effects of pornography this chapter attempts to suggest possible ways and means, by which one can stand against pornography, discard its desirability and get liberated from the bondage of pornographic addiction. Addressed to both those who are in bondage and those who are free, this chapter has focused primarily on pastoral care and pornography. Dealing with topics such as Pastor as helper, counseling a porn victim, breaking the porn addiction, etc., this chapter concludes with a brief common response to pornography. *Though some people in bondage tend to say that it is not possible to come out of the grips of pornographic addiction, they fail to see that nothing is impossible for God. He is able to deliver us and set us free from all kinds of bondages of the evil one. We only need to trust in his liberative work on the cross and obey His transforming Word.* Thus we are called and encouraged to give up our willing-slavery to pornography and to stand as the victorious people of a Holy and Righteous God.

This book has made us aware of the dark reality of pornography. This awareness must trouble our hearts and minds and enable us to see the noxious consequences of pornography and inspire and compel us to take a stand against it. The idea of sexual purity and holiness is vital for the welfare of our family, community and the society at large. We need to discard the false attractions of pornography, give up the willing slavery to this destructive evil and live a life of holiness as victorious people of a Holy God. We need to stand firm against every kind of filth and consciously promote purity in the context of sexual relationship, committing ourselves to follow whatever is truly good and honourable. *Let us not forget that the ugly proliferation of pornography is nourished by human weakness, spiritual lethargy, moral decay and a loss of human values. So we must constantly strive for excellence in our spirituality and morality in the context of our life and work.* We need to realize that to encounter the challenge of pornography is a challenge to be strong in our saving faith, determined in our serving commitment to God and to accelerate the task of evangelization, particularly among the youth. It is high time for us to make a difference by living a life of purity, integrity and responsibility in the context of a confused, perverted and permissive world.

Appendix 1

A Prayer and A Pledge

The Bible says, "Put off your old self, which is being corrupted by its deceitful desires; to be made new in the attitude of your minds; and to put on the new self, created to be like God in true righteousness and holiness" (Ephesians 4:22-24).

This describes a new life in God! You take off the old self and are made new by Jesus Christ. You submit Him your sinful nature, and He gives you His righteousness and holiness. You give Him your weakness, and He gives you His strength and power.

Pray this prayer sincerely and seriously:
"Dear Lord Jesus, I confess that I have sinned again and again. I feel trapped in bad habits, but I am reaching out to you in hope and faith. Thank You for dying on the cross for me. Please forgive me and grant me a new start today. I give myself to You and invite You to be the Lord of my life. Thank You for saving me from the power of sin and death. Now Lord, 'turn my eyes away from worthless things; preserve my life according to your word' (Pas 119:37). 'Create in me a pure heart, O God, and renew a steadfast spirit within me.' (Ps 51:10). Please fill me with Your Holy Spirit and give me Your power, wisdom and grace, so that I can obey You and walk according to Your ways every moment of my life. Thank you for answering my prayer. Amen."

Appendix 1

Now take this pledge:

"I made a covenant with my eyes not to look lustfully at a girl." – Job 31:1

Appendix 2

Check List for Sexual Addiction
(Based on Sex Addicts Anonymous Self Assessment Tool)

Answer the following questions to assess whether you may have a problem of sexual addiction:

1. Do you find yourself looking for sexually arousing pictures or articles in newspapers, magazines or Internet?
2. Do you keep secrets about your sexual or romantic activities from those important to you? Do you lead a double life in this regard?
3. Do you find that romantic or sexual fantasies interfere with your relationships or are preventing you from facing problems?
4. Do you feel shame about your body or your sexuality? Do you fear that you have no sexual feelings?
5. Do you look for more sex partners? Do you look for variety in sexual activities?
6. Do your sexual activities include the risk, threat, or reality of disease, pregnancy, coercion, or violence?
7. Have you ever been arrested to are you in danger of being arrested because of your practices of voyeurism, exhibitionism, prostitution, sex with minors, indecent phone calls, etc.?

8. Has your sexual or romantic behavior ever left you feeling hopeless, alienated from others, or suicidal?

9. Does your pursuit of sex or romantic relationships interfere with your spiritual beliefs or developments or social life?

If you answered "Yes" to even one of these questions, you need help. And help is available for all. See Appendix #3.

Appendix 3

Helpful Ministries and Organizations

Following is a list of significant ministries and organizations websites that could be helpful in providing information and assistance related to sexual issues including pornography.

MINISTRIES

Evangelical Outreach. A very helpful site with ample resources toward breaking the pornographic addiction, and to excel in personal spiritual growth.
Write: PO Box 265, Washington, PA 15301
Visit: www.evangelicaloutreach.org

Desert Stream Ministries. This ministry brings the healing power of Jesus to men and women struggling with sexual and relational issues such as homosexuality, sexual addiction, and sexual abuse.
Write: P.O. Box 17635, Anaheim, CA 92817-7635, 714-779-6899
Visit: www.DesertStream.org

What If? Freedom Ministries. This ministry is committed to assist others in escaping the grip of pornography.
Write: P.O. Box 470252, Tulsa, OK 74147-0252;
Call: +1-918-249-FREE (3733);
Visit: www.whatifministries.com

Sought Out, Inc. This ministry proclaims sexual redemption in Christ from pornography, adultery, and same-sex attraction.

Write: P.O. Box 62019, Virginia Beach, VA 23466;
Call: +1-757-631-0099;
Visit: www.soughtout.org

Faithful And True Ministries. This ministry features the resources on deliverance from sexual addiction.
Write: 6542 Regency Lane, Eden Prairie, MN 55344;
Visit: www.faithfulandtrueministries.com

Focus on the Family. This ministry features the resources of author Dr. James Dobson and other Christian experts on a myriad of topics including marriage, the family, pornography, and unfaithfulness.
Call: 800-A-FAMILY (232-6459);
Visit: www.family.org

Heart to Heart Counseling Centers. Features the resources of Dr. Douglas Weiss, a counselor, lecturer and author of such books as *Faithful and True: Sexual Integrity in a Fallen World* and *101 Practical Exercises for Sexual Addiction Recovery*.
Write: 5080 Mark Dabling Blvd., Colorado Springs, CO 80918;
Call: +1-719-278-3708;
Visit: www.sexaddict.com

Overcomers Outreach. This Christian-based addiction ministry uses a 12-step support group model.
Write: P.O. Box 2208, Oakhurst, CA 93644;
Call: 800-310-3001;
Visit: www.overcomersoutreach.org

Pure Life Ministries. This ministry offers the resources of author Steve Gallagher, plus residential care, phone counseling, help for wives of men in sexual sin, and Men of Purity Weekends.
Write: 14 School Street, Dry Ridge, KY 41035
Call: 877-301-7566
Visit: www.PureLifeMinistries.org

Theophostic Prayer Ministries

Pastors, professional counselors, and lay ministers use this method of prayer counseling to bring the healing power of Jesus to people with a wide variety of emotional wounds.
Write: P.O. Box 489, Campbellsville, KY 42719
Call: 270-465-3757
Visit: www.Theophostic.com

Christian Counseling
Visit: www.christiancounseling.cc

Pure Freedom/Setting Captives Free
Visit: www.settingcaptivesfree.com

ORGANIZATIONS (GROUPS AND NETWORKS)

Human Rights Law Network.
Write: 65 Masjid Road, 2nd Floor, Near DAV School Janpura, New Delhi;
Call: 011-24316922.

National Law Center for Children and Families.
This group is actively engaged in war on Porn.
Write: 3819 Plaza Dr. Fairfax, VA 22030-2512;
Call: +1- (703) 691-4626;
Visit: www.nationallawcenter.org

National Coalition for the Protection of Children and Families.
This group is actively engaged in war on Porn.
Write: 800 Compton Road, Suite 9224 Cincinnati, OH 45231;
Call: +1- (513) 521-6227;
Visit: www.nationalcoaltion.org

Morality in Media.
Write: 475 Riverside Dr., New York, NY 10115,
Call: +1-212-870-3222;
Visit: www.moralityinmedia.org

Community Defense Counsel
Write: 11000 N. Scottsdale Road, Suite 144, Scottsdale, AZ 85254,

Appendix 3   95

Call: (480) 922-9731;
Visit: www.communitydefense.org

Family Research Council.
Write: 801 G Street NW, Washington, DC 20001;
Call: +1- 202- 393-2100;
Visit: dianedew.com/porn.htm

eXXit. This website provides resources such as a daily three-minute Bible study to help those struggling with pornography to stand strong and resist temptation.
Visit: www.exxit.org

The Ford Foundation - The Ford Foundation is an American private foundation which has supported a number of studies and interventions in the area of sexuality and sexual behaviour.
Write: Programme Officer (Reproductive Health), Ford Foundation, 55 Lodhi Estate, New Delhi 110003.

Naz Foundation International (NFI) - NFI is headquartered in London, but works extensively in the South Asian region. Its mission is to ensure that issues of sexuality, sexual practices, and human rights concerns are addressed.
Write: NFI, 9, Gulzar Colony, New Berry Lane, Lucknow - 226001;
Call: 0522- 2205781; **Email:** arif@nfi.net; *Visit:* www.nfi.net

The Sexuality Information and Education Council of the U.S. (SIECUS) is a national, nonprofit organization which affirms that sexuality is a natural and healthy part of living. SIECUS develops, collects, and disseminates information, promotes comprehensive education about sexuality, and advocates the right of individuals to make responsible sexual choices.
Visit: www.siecus.org

Interventions for Support Healing and Awareness (IFSHA) –is working exclusively on sexuality and provides support in the form of Information material, Training programmes, Counseling services and so on. *Visit:* www.ifsha.org

TARSHI

Visit: **www.tarshi.org** – A very comprehensive website dealing with Indian realities including research, publications, Frequently Asked Questions, websites and events related to sexuality.

Sexuality Data

Visit: **www.sexualitydata.com** - An online sexual health encyclopedia about everything you have always wondered about, but were afraid to ask.

And many others...

Appendix 4

Suggested Readings

Addicted to "Love," by Stephen Arterburn, Servant Publications.

An Affair of the Mind By Laurie Hall

At the Altar of Sexual Idolatry, by Steve Gallagher, Pure Life Ministries.

Breaking Free: Understanding Sexual Addiction and the Healing Power of Jesus, by Russell Willingham, InterVarsity Press.

Every Man's Battle: Winning the War on Sexual Temptation One Victory at a Time, by Stephen Arterburn and Fred Stoeker with Mike Yorkey, Waterbrook Press.

Faithful and True: Sexual Integrity in a Fallen World, by Mark Laaser, Ph.D., Zondervan.

False Intimacy: Understanding the Struggle of Sex Addiction, by Dr. Harry Schaumburg, NavPress.

Ordering Your Private World, by Gordon MacDonald, Thomas Nelson Publishers.

Personal Holiness in Times of Temptation, by Bruce Wilkinson, Walk Thru the Bible Ministries.

Pure Desire: How One Man's Triumph Can Help Others Break Free From Sexual Temptation By Dr. Ted Roberts

Pure Freedom: Breaking the Addiction to Pornography by Mike Cleveland. Minnesota: Focus Publishing.

The Final Freedom: Pioneering Sexual Addiction Recovery, by Douglas Weiss, Ph.D., Heart to Heart Counseling Center.

Please look for more books in the bibliography.

Appendix 5

Suggestions for Further Research

Here is a list of suggestions outlined for further research/ study in relation to the issue of pornography.

1. This research has studied the issue of pornography basically from a religious perspective. It can also be studied and responded exclusively from biological, sociological, political, and psychological perspectives.
2. This work has been primarily limited to a Christian response to the issue of pornography. A research could also be undertaken on the responses of other religions, e.g., Hinduism, Buddhism, Islam, etc.
3. This research has not been able to focus largely on any case study or survey. A systematic research can be carried out to survey the production, consumption and criminal impacts of pornography in the Indian society.
4. To study in detail the issue of pornography in relation to various sexual issues and their implications such as, homosexuality, gender concerns, sex-works (both female and male prostitution), sex-crimes, etc., has not been possible in this research. A significant study could be undertaken in this area.
5. Pornography is primarily an attack on the dignity of women and children. Therefore it will be more appropriate if they, particularly women, raise their

voice against this evil with their personal feelings and reflections. In other words, women folks are suggested to engage in research on and response to the issue more than any other persons.

Bibliography

Books and resources marked with (*) are highly recommended for further reading on dealing with pornography.

Adams, Jay E. *A Theology of Christian Counseling: More Than Redemption.* Grand Rapids: Zondervan, 1979.

Anderson, Douglas A. *New Approaches to Family Pastoral Care.* Philadelphia: Fortress Press, 1980.

*Anderson, J. Kerby ed. *Living Ethically in the 90s.* Illinois: Victor Books, 1990.

*Arterburn, Stephen and Fred Stoeker with Mike Yorkey, *Every Man's Battle: Winning the War on Sexual Temptation One Victory at a Time.* Colorado: WaterBrook Press.

Arterburn, Stephen and Fred Stoeker with Mike Yorkey, *Every Young Man's Battle.* Colorado: WaterBrook Press, 2004.

Arterburn, Stephen and Jim Burns. *When Love is Not Enough: Parenting Through Tough Times.* Colorado: Focus on the Family, 1992.

Atkinson, David J. and David H. Field, eds. *New Dictionary of Christian Ethics and Pastoral Theology.* Leicester: Inter-Varsity Press, 1995.

Bayley, Anne. *One New Humanity: The Challenges of AIDS.* London: SPCK, 1996 and Delhi: ISPCK, 1998 reprint 2005.

Bowring, Lyndon ed., *Searching for Intimacy.* Bletchley, UK: Authentic Media, 2005.

Cassell. *Cassell's Dictionary of Sex Quotations.* London: Market House Books, 1993.

Cleveland, Mike. *Pure Freedom: Breaking the Addiction to Pornography.* Minnesota: Focus Publishing, 2002.

Cline, Victor. *Where Do You Draw the Line?* Utah: Brigham Young University Press, 1974.

Court, John H. *Pornography: A Christian Critique*. Illinois: InterVarsity Press, 1980.

Doniger, Simon, ed., *Sex and Religion Today*. New York: Association Press, 1953.

Falwell, Jerry. *The New American Family: The Rebirth of the American Dream*. Dallas: Word, 1992.

Gill, Margaret. *Free to Love: Sexuality and Pastoral Care*. Secunderabad: OM Books, 2004.

Graham-Murray, James. *A History of Morals*. London: Library 33 Limited, 1966.

Grenz, Stanely J. *Sexual Ethics: A Biblical Perspective*. Carlisle: Paternoster, 1990.

Griffiths, Richard. *Art, Pornography and Human Value: A Christian Approach to Violence and Eroticism in the Media*. Bramcote: Grove Books, 1975.

Grugni, Anthony. *Sex Education*. Mumbai: St Pauls, 2002.

Guruge, Ananda. *The Society of the Ramayana*. New Delhi: Abhinav Publications, 1991.

Hocking, David. *The Moral Catastrophe*. Oregon: Harvest House Publishers, 1990.

Jha, Harimohan. *Khattar Kaka*. New Delhi: Rajkamal Prakashan, 2001.

Kaitholil, George. *Marriage Call to Holiness*. Mumbai: St. Pauls, 2000.

Kennedy, Eugene. *The Unhealed Wound: The Church and Human Sexuality*. New York: St. Martin's, 2001.

Kuehne Dale S. *Sex and the iWorld: Rethinking Relationship beyond an Age of Individualism*. Grand Rapids: Bake Academic, 2009.

LaHaye, Tim. *The Act of Marriage*. Secunderabad: OM Books, 2004.

Lane, Pater. *Setting the Captives Free*. Milton, Australia: Exodus Asia Pacific, 2005.

Longford, Lord. *Pornography: The Longford Report*. London: Coronet Books, 1972.

Mabry, Hunter P. *A Manual for Researchers and Writers*. **Bangalore:** BTE-SSC, 1999.

Mabry, Hunter P. ed., *Christian Ethics: An Introductory Reader.* Serampore: ITL/SSC, 1987.

Mahendra, Shivraj K. *A Christian Response to Pornography.* Delhi: ISPCK, 2007.

McManus, Michael, ed., *Final Report of the Attorney General Commission on Pornography.* Nashville, Tennessee: Rutledge Hill Press, 1986.

Murray, John. *Collected Writings, Vol II.* Carlisle: Banner of Truth, 1978.

Olson, Jeff. *When A Man's Eye Wanders.* Grand Rapids: RBC Ministries, 1999.

Perry, Jason. *How Far Can You Go?* Mumbai: GLS Publishing, 2004.

Quay, Paul M. *The Christian Meaning of Human Sexuality.* San Francisco: Ignatius Press, 1985.

Robertson, A. T. *Word Pictures In The New Testament, Vol. VI.* New York: Harper, 1930.

Russell, Diana. *Rape and Marriage.* 1982.

Scanzoni, Letha. *Sex and the Single Eye.* Grand Rapids: Zondervan, 1968.

Smedes, Lewis B. *Sex for Christians: The Limits and Liberties of Sexual Living.* Grand

Rapids: William B. Eerdmans Pub. Co., 1976, reprint 1981.

Sonnenberg, Roger. *Human Sexuality: A Christian Perspective.* St. Louis, USA:Concordia Pub. House, 1998.

Stephen, M. *Introducing Christian Ethics.* Delhi: ISPCK, 2003.

Stott, John. *Issues Facing Christians Today.* Bombay: GLS, 1996.

The American *Presidential Commission Report on Obscenity and Pornography, 1970.*

Zacharias, Ravi. *Sense and Sensuality.* Chennai: RZIM Life Focus Society, 2003.

Articles and Periodicals

"Is Pornography a touchstone of a free society?" *Sunday Times of India,* Pune, August 15, 2004.

Althaus-Reid, Marcella Maria. "A Woman's Right to Not Being Straight (*El Derecho a no ser Derecha*): On Theology, Church and Pornography" *Concilium*, Vol. 2, 2002.

Bamzai, Kaveree and Unnithan, Sandeep. "The Seedy Drive" *India Today*, November 29, 2004.

Chandrakumar, M. "How to Overcome Online Temptation" *Light of Life*, August 2004.

Desai, Santosh. "The New Pornographies" *The Week*, September 25, 2005.

Donnerstein, Edward. "Pornography and Violence Against Women" *Annal of the New York Academy of Science* 347 (1980).

Dubey, Bharati K. "Indian Society Comes To Terms With Sex Sleaze," *The Movie Age*, August 6, 2004.

India Today, November 8, 2004.

India Today, December 15, 1978.

India Today, December 5, 2011.

India Today, February 27, 2012.

Kantzer, Kenneth. "The Power of Porn" *Christianity Today*, February 7, 1986.

Kazmi, Nikhat & O'brien, Allen. "Legalise Porn?" *Times News Network*, Tuesday, July 12, 2005.

Kazmi, Nikhat. "Why Sex Helps Tech Sell..." *Pune Times*, August 2, 2005.

Kennedy, D. James and Graham, Franklin, "Ten Ways to Break the Stronghold of Pornography" *Forerunner*, June 2005.

Khare, Varun. "Snailed by Pornography" *AIM*, July 2004.

Mahendra, Shivraj K. "A Feminist Study of Selected Texts in the Bible," (Unpublished paper, United Theological College, Bangalore, November 2010), p. 5.

Minnick, Liz. "Pornography" *Home Life*, 1994.

Murphy, Paul J. "Pornography, Promiscuity, Perversion" *Homiletic & Pastoral Review*, Vol. 89, No. 3, December 1988.

Nalunnakkal, George Mathew. "The Indian Church and the Sacred Cow of Human Sexuality" *National Council of Churches Review*, May 2001.

Outlook, December 26, 2011

Sherkat, Darren E. and Ellison, Christopher G. "The Cognitive Structure of a Moral Crusade: Conservative Protestantism and Opposition to Pornography" *Social Forces* 75:3, March 1997.

Stein, Dan J., et.al., "Hypersexual Disorder and Preoccupation with Internet Pornography" *The American Journal of Psychiatry Vol. 158 (10)* October 2001.

The Daily Mail, London, August 14, 2004.

Thomas, Sean. "Self Abuse" *The Spectator*, June 28, 2003.

Vincent, Arvin "Rape City Gets Inspiration From Rape Porn" *Hindustan Times*, Tuesday, September 27, 2005.

Zillman, Bryant, Carveth, "The Effect of Erotica Featuring Sadomasochism and Beastiality on Motivated Inter-Male Aggression," *Personality and Social Psychology Bulletin* 7 (1981).

Zillman, Dolf and Bryant, Jennings. "Pornography, Sexual Callousness, and the Trivialization of Rape," *Journal of Communication* 32 (1982).

Online Articles and Weblinks

"Pornography and Ethics" http://www.muslimphilosophy.com.

"Ten Steps To Freedom In Christ" http://www.cbn.com/spirituallife/CBNTeaching-Sheets/Pornography.asp (January 15, 2006).

"Tricks Pornographers Play" http://internet-filterreview.toptenreviews.com/tricks-pornographers-play.html.

Lasley, D. Marty "A Theology of Pornography: Is There Anything Wrong With Nudie Pictures?" http://www.americanwasteland.com (January 15, 2006).

Pellauer, Mary. "Pornography: An Agenda for the Churches," http://www.religion-online.org (November 6, 2005), www.christiancentury.org (January 15, 2006).

Peters, Robert. "The Link Between Pornography and Violent Sex Crimes" http://www.moralityinmedia.org.

Asian Sex Gazette http://www.*AsianSexGazette.com*.

Bible Questions http://www.biblequestions.org/Archives/BQAR386.htm

Bibliography

Billy Graham Answers http://www.billygraham.org/MyAnswer_Article.asp?ArticleID=2437

Care Organization http://www.care.org.uk/group/group.aspx?id=17169.

Christian Century http://www.christiancentury.org.

Christian Doctrine http://www.christiandoctrine.net.

Dalitstan http://www.dalitstan.org/books/awake.html.

*Evangelical Outreach http://www.evangelicaloutreach.org.

Geocities http://www.geocities.com/Athens/Agora/4229.html.

*Gospel Net http://www.gospelnet.org.

*Got Questions http://www.gotquestions.org/pornography-Bible.html

Internet Filter Review http://www.internet-filter-review.toptenreviews.com/internet-pornography-statistics.html.

Morality in Media http://www.moralityinmedia.org.

Obscenity Crimes http://www.obscenitycrimes.org.

Padfield http://www.padfield.com.

Probe http://www.probe.org.

Pure Intimacy http://www.pureintimacy.org/cs/couples/a0000094.cfm

Religion Online http://www.religion-online.org.

Sex Addicts Recovery http://www.saa_recovery.org

Sahayog India http://www.sahayogindia.org.

Scripture Essay http://www.scripturessay.com/q511a.html

Traditional Values http://www.traditionalvalues.org.

Electronic Resources

Compton's Interactive Encyclopedia Deluxe © 1998 The Learning Company, Inc.

Hornby, A. S. ed., Oxford Advanced Genie, *Oxford Advanced Learner's Dictionary of Current English*, 6th Edition Oxfrod: Oxford University Press, 2000.

Pappas, Theodore, ed., *Encyclopedia Britannica 2004 Ultimate Reference Suite CD*, Encyclopedia Britannica *Dictionary*, Encyclopedia Britannica, Inc.

OTHER WORKS BY THE AUTHOR

Books

A Christian Response to Pornography (2007)

Masih Meri Manzil (2008)

Hindi Translations

Timothy C. Tennent, *Christianity at the Religious Roundtable* (Baker, USA, 2002), as *Dharmik Golmej Par Masihiyat* (Delhi: ISPCK, 2003).

Premraj Dharmanand, *Your Questions - Our Answers* (Dehradun: Author, 2003), as *Apke Sawal - Hamare Jawab* (Dehradun: Author, 2003). Both English and Hindi versions in one cover.

C. B. Firth, *An Introduction to Indian Church History* (Madras: CLS, 1961), as *Bhartiya Kalisiya Ka Itihas Ek Parichaya* (Dehradun: NTC, 2006, Revised 2009).

Peter Horrobin, *The Most Powerful Prayer on Earth* (Secunderabad: OM Books, 2005), as *Preethwee Par Sabse Shaktishali Prarthana* (in Press).

O. L. Snaitang, *A History of Ecumenical Movement: An Introduction* (Bangalore: SATHRI, 2004), as *Sarwabhaumik Andolan Ka Itihas: Ek Parichay* (Dehradun: NTC, 2008).

Scott D. Allen, et. al., *The Worldview of the Kingdom of God.* (AZ: FHI, 2003), as *Parmeshwar Ke Rajya Ka Drishtikon* (New Delhi: SALT-EFI, 2010).

M. M. Thomas, *The Acknowledge Christ of the Indian Renaissance* (Madras: CLS, 1970), as *Bharteey Punarjagaran Ka Abhisweekrit Masih* (Dehradun: NTC, 2010).

Darrow L. Miller, et. al., *God's Unshakable Kingdom* (Seat tle: YWAM, 2005), as *Parmeshwar Ka Atal Rajya* (New Delhi: SALT-EFI, 2012).

Jeff Jones, Bruice Miller et al., *Discovering the Christian Life* (Texas: CCBT, 2002). as *Masihi Jeevan Kee Khoj* (in Press).

CBSI, *Community Bible Study International: Bible Study Lessons* (Colorado Springs: CBS International, 2011). *(in Progress).*

Contact the Author

*I would love to hear from you:
Please get in touch. Thank you.*

Shivraj Mahendra
Mobile: 91-9410-531-001
E-mail: shivrajkm@gmail.com
Blog: www.shivrajmahendra.blogspot.com
Facebook: www.facebook.com/shivraj.mahendra

www.ingramcontent.com/pod-product-compliance
Lightning Source LLC
Chambersburg PA
CBHW032128090426
42743CB00007B/507